ARCHITECTURE 04

ARCHITECTURE 04
THE GUIDE TO
THE RIBA AWARDS

EDITED BY TONY CHAPMAN

RIBA

MERRELL
LONDON · NEW YORK

500

First published 2004 by Merrell Publishers Limited

Head office: 42 Southwark Street, London SE1
Telephone +44 (0)20 7403 2047
E-mail mail@merrellpublishers.com

New York office: 49 West 24th Street, 8th Floor, New York, NY 10010
Telephone +1 212 929 8344
E-mail info@merrellpublishersusa.com

www.merrellpublishers.com

PUBLISHER Hugh Merrell
US DIRECTOR Joan Brookbank
EDITORIAL DIRECTOR Julian Honer
MANAGING EDITOR Anthea Snow
EDITOR Sam Wythe
DESIGN MANAGER Nicola Bailey

JUNIOR DESIGNER Paul Shinn
PRODUCTION MANAGER Michelle Draycott
PRODUCTION CONTROLLER Sadie Butler
SALES AND MARKETING DIRECTOR Emilie Amos
SALES AND MARKETING EXECUTIVE Emily Sanders

British Library Cataloguing-in-Publication Data:
Chapman, Tony, 1953–
Architecture 04 : the guide to the RIBA awards
1.Architecture – Awards – Great Britain 2.Architecture – Europe – 21st century
I.Title II.Royal Institute of British Architects
720.9′4′09051
ISBN 1 85894 260 8

Produced by Merrell Publishers Limited
Edited by Tom Neville
Designed by Claudia Schenk

Printed and bound in Great Britain

CONTENTS

BLOBS, SPIKES AND SHARDS

In the architectural press the talk has been of blobs, but spikes and shards were also represented on this year's Stirling shortlist. Like the nineteenth-century railway companies, the RIBA seems to have three classes of awards: Stirling, Special and RIBA. Of course, it's not like that at all: each is different and all are equal. So, far from flying Concorde with the Stirling judges, whose ages ranged from 73 years (architect Ted Cullinan) to five weeks (Ned Allen, non-voting son of *Architects' Journal* editor Isabel Allen) – the others being Dutch architect Francine Houben, dancer Deborah Bull and sculptor Antony Gormley – we enjoyed Ryanair's hospitality (muffins or KitKats) instead. Nor is it all buses and minicabs for the judges of the RIBA Awards (the first stage of the long process leading to Stirling): this year's Scottish judges were flown by helicopter to the north coast to see a house that finally failed to get an award – how rigorous is that? For once, though, this is not to be an essay on the judging of Stirling but rather a celebration of those relatively unsung prizes, the Special Awards. Nor is it meant to be an essay on transport (though I will try to persuade RIBA President George Ferguson to lend the Wessex jury his Routemaster bus next year).

The Special Awards have grown out of the old category awards, the winners of which were automatically stuck on the Stirling shortlist. This gave a balanced (by type) but sometimes skewed (in terms of quality) list from which the Stirling judges had to choose. Three of those categories have survived: Client of the Year; the Stephen Lawrence Prize – whose definition of small has veered from £500,000 to £100,000 before settling on £350,000; and the Manser Medal for the best house (a reincarnation of the earlier, inelegantly titled Houses and Housing Award). There are now seven awards, with other claimants such as regeneration, urbanism and collaborative working clamouring in the wings. All seven are presented on the occasion of Stirling, with Manser having muscled past the others to get itself on television alongside the big one, largely as a result of presenter Kevin McCloud's special interest in the subject. It even gets four post-*Channel 4 News* slots to itself in the run-up to the Stirling presentation. For the first time the presentation was broadcast live (as a former producer of both live and pre-recorded programmes, I know how frightening this is), the production company, Talkback, having bitten the bullet previously eschewed by Waldemar Januszczak's ZCZ.

Each of the special awards has its own expert jury plus, in all but a couple of cases, me. First up this year was the new RIBA Inclusive Design Award, replacing the ADAPT Trust Access Award. Over the past four years Stewart Coulter and I have peered into dozens of disabled toilets – perhaps that should be accessible toilets; most public toilets seem to be disabled. This year I had new companions, new sponsors: Sarah Langton-Lockton of the Centre for Accessible Environments, which takes a broader view of the issue, widening the prize's remit to designing all buildings for all people; and Mike Hield of the architectural ironmongers Allgood, a man who understands the buildings his products go into and help make work. We visited a shortlist of four. The Allies and Morrison extension to and refurbishment of the Horniman Museum was the first to be seen. Its excellence in these terms at least is somewhat compromised by the acoustics of its new entrance and by the low light levels in one of the galleries. On to Manchester to see OMI's Chinese Arts Centre. This scored highly on inclusiveness, in that it brings Chinese culture to a broad audience, but is let down by awkward access – in effect insisted upon by the planners – and by the artist's studio reached only by ladder – very Chinese but hardly within the spirit of the Disability Discrimination Act, the final duties in Part 3 having just come into force. Ian Simpson's brilliant achievement in linking five existing buildings at Manchester Museum above and below ground is qualified only by a number of awkward internal junctions.

Our final shortlisted scheme, the City of Manchester Stadium, was hard to fault. Built for the Commonwealth Games, the first in which events for disabled athletes were integrated into the main competition, this had accessibility, as well as adaptability, designed in from the outset. We were shown round by Manchester City Council's access officer, a lifelong Manchester City supporter and a wheelchair user himself. Instead of being corralled in a pitch-level pen open to the elements as he was at Maine Road, he now has one of the best views in the place and can sit next to able-bodied or disabled friends. His enthusiasm for the project is infectious – a clear winner.

The next visits were to the five schemes shortlisted for the Crown Estate Conservation Award, and overlapped with the Inclusive Design visits, as the Manchester Museum was on both lists. My fellow judges were Richard Griffiths, cathedral architect at Southwark and St Albans and a member of the RIBA Awards Group; David Pickles, senior architect in English Heritage's Conservation Department; and Giles Worsley, architecture critic of *The Daily Telegraph*. We were looking for the best restoration or adaptation of a building that is itself of some architectural significance. The addition to the Manchester Museum is beautifully handled – a lead-clad entrance hall both complements and links the old buildings – but we were less convinced by the hands-off approach to the pure conservation work. Similarly, at Compton Verney we were more impressed by the clarity of Stanton Williams's new work than by the treatment of the old house, where there seemed to be some indecision as to whether they were inserting a gallery into a country house or restoring a country house that contained a gallery. Sker House by Davies Sutton was a remarkable project: a mainly sixteenth-century house of which part had been left as a stabilized ruin, part roofed as a camping-out space, and part fully roofed and converted into a family home. Though an excellent repair, doubts remained about the design of fittings, flooring and services. Grange Park Opera House is remarkable and works best where least has been done – in particular the house used for dining, where magical nets have been stretched to catch any falling plaster, and the rooms dressed with theatrical props – or where most had been done – in the opera house where netting is again used but where the stage is expressed on the outside as a simple timber and concrete box. We were less happy about the reconstruction of the link between the main house and the orangery, based on the early nineteenth-century original.

Any of the three might have been winners in a less good year, but HOK's sensitive and imaginative work in bringing new life and purpose to the King's Library at the British Museum was a clear winner. A product of close working with the museum's own curators and designers, this faultless piece of conservation has revealed the room in its full glory as one of the finest in London. Intervention in the historic fabric appears at first glance to be minimal, yet the more you look the more you become aware of the work that has gone into the project. The whole room has been invisibly serviced and beautifully lit, employing great ingenuity in hiding 200 kilometres of wiring.

After three awards involving long journeys by train and car, it was a welcome change to gather at the RIBA to consider shortlists for the two awards that do not generally involve further visits: Sustainability and Client of the Year. Sponsored this year for the first time by Schüco, the curtain-wall people, the Sustainability Award was judged by experts Bill Gething, who chairs the RIBA Sustainable Futures Committee, and Bill Dunster, last year's winner, together with Awards Group chair, Eric Parry, and myself. We looked at four schemes and their environmental credentials, which ranged from twenty pages to a few lines. Bill Dunster kicked things off by suggesting that the RIBA should not have a sustainability award at all; if a building's not green it shouldn't have won an award in the first place. Up to a point. ... And it's OK for him, he's already won his. Eric declared that off the agenda and we set about eliminating Lifschutz Davidson's Davidson House – an admirable environmental strategy and a benchmark for all new offices, but not quite exemplary – and Limerick County Hall – a public building for which the same could be said, though it sets a standard that national and local government in the UK should be aiming for.

So the panel agreed there were only two major contenders: Beaufort Court – an egg farm beside the M25, converted by Studio E into the offices of a company called Zero Emissions, which generates more energy via its wind turbine than it consumes – and Stock Orchard Street – a small live-work development by Sarah Wigglesworth for herself and her partner, Jeremy Till, on the site of some redundant workshops close to London's Caledonian Road. The egg-farm conversion incorporates the very latest renewable-energy installations, including a large wind turbine highly visible from the motorway, and is understood to be the first carbon-neutral office in the UK. This project represents the most thorough application of both low- and zero-carbon technologies, and is exemplary in many respects, providing the large car park and loss of potentially productive agricultural land are overlooked. The panel also felt that the conversion to high-technology modern office space, though imaginative, was not perhaps the most appropriate use of the historic farm buildings. A straight choice, then, between a building that ticked all the boxes and one that left a number of them blank, but that excited the judges far more architecturally. In the end we decided to congratulate Beaufort Court on its engineering excellence, but give the award to Stock Orchard Street.

The day following the sustainability judging, the Awards Group met to choose the RIBA/Arts Council England Client of the Year. Although they pick the final six from which the Stirling winner is chosen, this is the only winner they themselves choose – a small compensation for all the donkey work they get through (trips to Austria, Greece, Germany, Sweden, Holland, etc.). All agree this was the strongest list ever. There's an unwritten rule that the award should go for 'repeat business', that is, to a client with a track record to prove it's no fluke. Eric Parry, as chair, knew the work of the Kielder Partnership in Northumberland and threw *Skyspace*, an artwork by James Turrell, into an already rich mix of Nick Coombe and Shona Kitchen's Minotaur (a maze) and Softroom's Belvedere. Together, these schemes have made for a great visitor experience but they don't quite stack up against the scale of achievement of some of the opposition. The Coventry Phoenix Initiative qualifies because of the breadth of the art and architecture projects – not to mention their long gestation period – and the effect they have had in transforming this tired quarter of the city. Chris Beck, the client, hugely impressed the Stirling midlist judges as a man for whom 'public service' are not dirty words and who has dedicated much of his life to improving the public realm. But again, not quite enough in this tough field. Selfridges have done some great commissioning, in London and Manchester as well as in Birmingham (a building that many expected to see on the Stirling shortlist). But the man behind the commissions, Vittorio Radice, has gone and a number of planned projects have been cancelled – perhaps not quite the right message. The Maggie's Centres are wonderful in concept and execution, with completed buildings from Richard Murphy, Page and Park and, this year, Frank Gehry with James F Stephen, and more to come from Richard Rogers, Daniel Libeskind and Zaha Hadid. So their chance will come again, and surely one day Laura Lee, who was Maggie Jencks's nurse and the inspiration behind the cancer-care centres, will be up on stage collecting the award.

The clear winner was The Peabody Trust for its pioneering work in three centuries, culminating in their highly influential and experimental work with modular construction at Murray Grove, by Cartwright Pickard, and this year at Raines Court, by Allford Hall Monaghan Morris, the largest volumetric scheme for shared ownership built to date. It's appropriate timing, too, with Dickon Robinson going part-time at the Trust. But the good work goes on, with a new joint project with Arup, Project Meteor, in which they are working with the private sector to produce concrete volumetric housing in a factory.

This year I took no role in judging two of the awards. *The Architects' Journal* First Building Award was judged by Barrie Evans, *AJ*'s buildings' editor, co-sponsor Robin Ellis, and last year's winner, Alex de Rijke. They visited The Black House, of which more later; Double House – the most luxurious back-to-back ever, a pair of all-brick houses designed for two brothers and their families – and In-Between, two houses and two flats in a terrace of three dwellings designed and built by Annalie Riches, Silvia Ullmayer and Barti Garibaldo. This innovative and delightful terrace was unanimously agreed to be the winner, and the judges praised it for being rich in terms of space, light, ambition and resolution, despite its low budget.

The Stephen Lawrence Prize was judged this year by its sponsor, RIBA past-President Marco Goldschmied, Doreen Lawrence, mother of the murdered teenager, who has subsequently come to share her son's passion for architecture, and journalist David Taylor. They went to see The Black House (again, more later); La Concha, designed by MOOArc for the architect and his family in Guernsey; In-Between; and Vista, the black-rubber-clad house by Simon Condor in the wilds of Dungeness, the unanimously agreed winner.

The final award, and the only special award to be seen by Channel 4 viewers, was the Manser Medal, judged by the eponymous RIBA past-President, Jamie Fobert, last year's winner, Michael Hanson, editor of co-sponsor *Best of British Homes*, David Birkbeck of Design for Homes, and myself. We spent two days in the south and east of England, covering 800 kilometres. On the first day we saw The Black House (of which there were actually two, the other being Vista – these days architects are not content simply to dress in black; they seem to insist on a similar dress code for their houses). Architect-owner Meredith Bowles must have been sick of the sight of RIBA judges by now and probably deserved an award for persistence alone. The Black House sits on eight piles above the Cambridgeshire Fens, speaking the language of indigenous barns. On to James Gorst's exquisite Wakelins, his fifth commission for an American banker client, who was surprised to find his property was listed until they peeled back the façade of an undistinguished 1950s house to discover a row of Tudor cottages underneath. These Gorst has restored and reclad, and added an oak-clad box that complements the remainder in scale if not in style. And so on to Dungeness, where it feels as though the world has ended. England certainly has – maybe something to do with the nuclear power station near by. This black house is clad in the kind of rubber divers don, the sort that breathes. Stepping through the porch, made from a hut already on the site, you enter a world of plywood: walls, floors, ceilings and all the fixtures. The joinery has the quality of a luxury-yacht's fittings, and this is completely appropriate to its setting amid the wild, flat expanses of Dungeness. Looking out through the fully glazed doors on to the deck at the passing shipping, you feel as if you are at sea yourself, in a timber cocoon safe from the billowing gales.

A lively discussion ensued on the way back, before it came down to a straight choice between Vista and The Black House. In the end it was third time lucky for Meredith Bowles and his Black House, partly because of what it has to say to housebuilders at a time when the government is calling for more and more homes to be built, and partly because of its immaculate green credentials. As with all these awards, all the contenders were special; but some were more special than others.

In some ways judging all the special awards makes Stirling seem like a doddle. The Stirling judges just have to pick one from six. But it still takes four days of five very busy people's time. And there are the inevitable non-running Stansted Expresses, flights cancelled, 4 a.m. starts and taxis not turning up, avoiding Dublin night life because of that same 4 a.m. start, trying to find places to eat on a Sunday night in Graz, a city that closes at 8 p.m., Manchester in the rain, a rainbow seen from the top of the Gherkin, good conversation, gossip and laughter, a lot of food, plenty to drink and not much sleep – and some fine architecture, too. Plus a final get together at the RIBA on the day of the presentation to come up with a winner, with the help of a secret ballot.

And so another year's judging and presentations have come to a close in October. We can rest on our laurels until December, when it all begins again.

11 .BLOBS, SPIKES AND SHARDS

THE STIRLING PRIZE

IN ASSOCIATION WITH THE ARCHITECTS' JOURNAL

The RIBA Stirling Prize, now in its ninth year, is for the fourth year sponsored by *The Architects' Journal* and is awarded to the architects of the building thought to be the most significant of the year for the evolution of architecture and the built environment. It is the UK's richest and most prestigious architectural prize. The winners receive a cheque for £20,000 and a trophy, which they hold for one year.

The prize is named after the architect Sir James Stirling (1926–1992), one of the most important British architects of his generation and a progressive thinker and designer throughout his career. He is best known for his Leicester University Engineering Building (1959–63), the Staatsgallerie in Stuttgart (1977–84), and his posthumous Number One Poultry building in London. His former partner, Michael Wilford, won the 1997 Stirling Prize for the jointly designed Stuttgart Music School, and in 2003 year won an RIBA Award for the History Museum that completed Stirling's masterplan for the Stuttgart Staatsgalerie complex.

The winner of the 2004 RIBA Stirling Prize in association with *The Architects' Journal* was 30 ST MARY AXE.

30 ST MARY AXE
.LONDON EC3 .FOSTER AND PARTNERS

This is the first office building to win the RIBA Stirling Prize and the first to be voted for unanimously by the judges, who were keen to stress the key role played by the Swiss Re client, Sarah Fox.

Swiss Re wanted a landmark building and Foster and Partners have certainly given them one. But they have not just got a shiny new logo for their previously low-profile reinsurance business; they also have a building that is already loved by Londoners. Seven thousand people joined queues up to three-quarters-of-a-mile long during Open House London to get inside, and as many again were turned away disappointed. Those who got to the top may have been disappointed, too: this is the only vantage point in London from which you cannot see the Gherkin.

As this 40-storey tapering building is already a popular icon on the City skyline, the jury tended to concentrate on the degree to which this iconic structure did in fact provide a pay-off in terms of facility, ambience and interpretation of the basic mathematics of the project.

The architects describe 30 St Mary Axe as 'the capital's first environmentally progressive tall building'. And indeed it takes many of the ideas about naturally ventilated high-rises – such as drawing fresh air through the light wells that spiral up the building – from the same practice's Commerzbank in Frankfurt. The winding-round of these spaces is played against two other moves: the tapering of the tower (the obvious factor in its being dubbed 'the gherkin'), and the decision to offer lessees 'six-pack' or 'two-pack' options – that is, units of six or two floors. The light wells are triangular on plan and six of them divide the otherwise continuous ring of offices on each floor into six segments. Each of these roughly rectangular segments therefore benefits from being close to a pair of spiralling voids (whether of two or six storeys). This system is modified at the upper floors, where the building's geometry starts to squeeze in, creating some interesting spaces.

What this complex three-dimensional geometry achieves for the building is

CLIENT SWISS RE
STRUCTURAL ENGINEER ARUP
SERVICES ENGINEER HILSON MORAN PARTNERSHIP LTD
LIGHTING DESIGNER SPEIRS AND MAJOR ASSOCIATES
QS GARDINER & THEOBALD
MAIN CONTRACTOR SKANSKA CONSTRUCTION UK LTD
CONTRACT VALUE CONFIDENTIAL
COMPLETION DATE OCTOBER 2003
GROSS INTERNAL AREA 46,000 SQUARE METRES (OFFICE/RETAIL)
PHOTOGRAPHER GRANT SMITH/NIGEL YOUNG/FOSTER AND PARTNERS

not only clever, but also intelligent. The light wells, in addition to breaking up the office areas into well-proportioned chunks and providing atria and spatial interest, primarily serve to bring light and air right into the depth of the building. The office areas work equally well, whether open-plan or sub-divided with glass walls.

One side of the office zone adjacent to a light well is offered as a communal service area. Usually – and particularly in high-rise developments – such areas are relegated to some windowless corner. Here, by contrast, whether socializing, photocopying or making tea, staff can benefit from magnificent views of the City at their feet.

The architects have made the most of the benefits of the tapering volume at pedestrian level. In earlier versions of this scheme the building took up the whole site; now the reduction in the building's girth at ground level allows through routes, which help to knit the City back together. Also, the relatively small footprint of a circular building frees up additional precious ground space for landscaping. Low walls and seats marking the historic boundaries of the site define a public plaza giving safe access to the double-height shops at ground-floor level. The aerodynamic form also means that down-draughts are less than those generated by a rectilinear building, further increasing the comfort of the public. Another effect of the tapering form is that, close up, it is impossible to take in the whole of the structure, so that the bulk one would usually associate with a 46,000-square-metre building is greatly reduced.

Internally, the ground-floor lift lobby is suitably elegant, and the bar area at the top responds to the challenge and opportunity of elevation, situation and view, making it one of the very best rooms in twenty-first-century London. At last the city is getting back the vantage points it deserves. If only it could be publicly accessible …

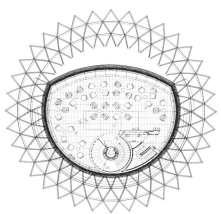

LEVEL 40 FLOOR PLAN

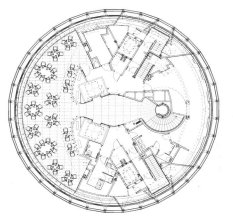

LEVEL 39 FLOOR PLAN

THE BUSINESS ACADEMY BEXLEY
.ERITH .FOSTER AND PARTNERS

A business academy doesn't sound like a lot of fun, but this one is. It's a very special and different school that would not look out of place in a business park. The high-risk strategy of offering students aged 11 to 18 such a traditionally adult building form seems to have paid off: apparently a group of students who had trashed their previous classroom arrived at their new school voluntarily wearing suits. Of course there was a touch of irony about it, but since then they've come to thrive on the respect the building pays them.

Foster and Partners have turned their facility with offices to the world of education and come up with a school where results are proving that good architecture makes people's lives better. The Business Academy Bexley does what ground-breaking architecture ought to do: it makes you rethink the function of the building. Here the educational and architectural thinking go hand in hand. It does not look ground-breaking, but its unflamboyant exterior contains a stylish world of three-storey streets and squares in which nearly all walls are transparent. Organization is legible and deceptively simple, incorporating spaces such as the theatre, which are usually given special architectural treatment, undemonstratively into the whole.

It is a ruthlessly simple box with east and west façades protected by moveable vertical louvres – a neat solution to an otherwise unfavourable classroom orientation and adding greatly to security: the shutters close automatically at dusk, turning it into a vandal-proof box. Inside, this is about as open-plan as a school can get. Early reports suggest that teachers and students have responded well to this layout. The problems of previous hybrid school models that combined closed classrooms and open study areas are not in evidence here. Even the classrooms with walls, such as the science laboratories, are predominantly glazed, and this contributes further to the sense of openness and community.

Apart from the sophisticated external louvres, the environmental-control systems are simple and the overall efficiency of building form should make this a relatively low-energy building.

CLIENT GARRARD EDUCATIONAL TRUST
SPONSORS SIR DAVID AND LADY GARRARD
STRUCTURAL ENGINEER BURO HAPPOLD
QS DAVIS LANGDON
CONTRACTOR EXTERIOR INTERNATIONAL PLC
CONTRACT VALUE CONFIDENTIAL
COMPLETION DATE AUGUST 2003
GROSS INTERNAL AREA 11,800 SQUARE METRES
PHOTOGRAPHER NIGEL YOUNG

The building plan is flexible and extendable, and seems to be working well as a venue for a wide variety of out-of-school-hours activity by students and by the community. If the treatment of the exterior landscape follows the same level of ambition and clarity, a very good building could be transformed into a great one.

The business academy appears to be a bold first step in transforming its desolate surroundings and restoring pride to the local community. The old school, boarded up and graffitied (and undoubtedly the alma mater of the models for *Clockwork Orange*'s Droogs), sits moodily to the side awaiting demolition, a part of the Thamesmead experiment soon to be erased. Next door, the future of education is shiny, even a little corporate, but also humane, and this is reflected in the vast collage in the main entrance atrium that comprises individual portrait photographs of every student.

It feels as if it cost more to build than most schools, and it did, though not dramatically more. But at the same time it is cheaper to run, in terms of both energy and maintenance. This may seem surprising, with all that glass necessitating a daily cleaning regime. However, because there are almost no secret places, there is also no vandalism to repair, or graffiti to remove. And there is dramatically less bullying. So perhaps one of the lessons this building teaches us is that school buildings should not be too cheap. This is a building which demonstrates respect for its population of underprivileged pupils and for its staff, and receives their respect in return.

It is a building that should touch each of their lives. It is also a building that suggests a radical new future for the way education is delivered. Bexley may not quite be a universal answer, and it might be a very different story with another head and different staff. But if any building can teach the value of the collaboration of client and architect, and indeed the social value of architecture, this one can.

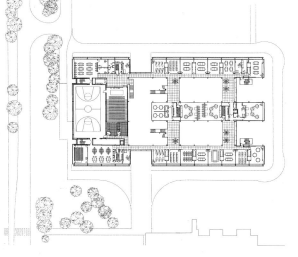

SITE PLAN

22 .STIRLING PRIZE

IMPERIAL WAR MUSEUM NORTH
.MANCHESTER .STUDIO DANIEL LIBESKIND

The Imperial War Museum North was built to house some of the London museum's unseen collections and bring them to new audiences in the north; but it does far more than that. As the client Jim Forrester points out, the commission presented a triple challenge: to overcome contemporary distaste for things imperial, for anything to do with war, and for museums themselves. Daniel Libeskind has risen brilliantly to the challenge with his physical commentary on the pity of war in the form of the shards of a shattered globe. Sitting on the banks of the Manchester Ship Canal, its skewed tower marks the entrance to an extraordinary exhibition that honours the dead of twentieth-century conflicts without glorifying war. Three audio-visual shows transfix audiences with images of war and the voices of its participants and victims. This is architectural theatre at its very best.

The promoters of this £20 million building took a huge risk in selecting and developing a design by an architect who at the time had only one completed building to his name; and they got a lot for their money. The director has worked in many museums and is delighted to be running a new one without the constraints imposed on so many by their often listed but totally unsuitable buildings. While from the outside the building is an extrovert and flamboyant response to the dereliction of the site, the most remarkable achievement of the design is the ease with which one moves or flows around this apparently jarring and jagged series of shapes.

The architect's highlighting of the poetry of the three shards almost blinds us to its practicalities, like the clever way in which the main floor is raised up to the first floor to minimize impact on the contaminated site and to provide vast external (and therefore low-cost) plant rooms in the undercroft. These are places of great beauty in their own right: the permeable gravel floors, which allow for any methane seepage, have the air of a Japanese garden, while overhead the services are cased in stainless steel and are as neat as a circuit diagram.

CLIENT TRUSTEES IMPERIAL WAR MUSEUM NORTH
ASSOCIATE ARCHITECT LEACH RHODES WALKER
EXHIBITION DESIGN REAL STUDIOS LTD
AV CONSULTANT EVENT COMMUNICATIONS
LIGHTING DHA DESIGN
STRUCTURAL ENGINEER ARUP
SERVICES ENGINEER CONNELL MOTT MACDONALD
QS TURNER & TOWNSEND GRP
CONTRACTOR SIR ROBERT MCALPINE LTD
CONTRACT VALUE £19.7 MILLION
COMPLETION DATE MAY 2002
GROSS INTERNAL AREA 9000 SQUARE METRES
PHOTOGRAPHER BITTER BREDT FOTOGRAFIE

There is no doubt that, as intended, the building disorientates the visitor; even the entrance is not where one might suppose, facing the footbridge leading from the Lowry, but on the Trafford side. Once through the door, you are in an inside-outside space, the Air Shard Tower, which is clad in extruded box-section planks. In the main hall the objects sit on the gently and irregularly raking floor among the fractured rhomboids that contain within them separate exhibitions linked by a timeline; their external walls provide projection surfaces for 'the big show' with 60 projectors.

The principal spaces – the main hall, the temporary exhibition gallery and the restaurant – are all cathedral-like volumes with hard surfaces, yet the acoustics are not unpleasant. The daylight in the restaurant provides welcome relief, as do the calm day-lit education rooms.

A £10 million budget cut meant not only that was one whole shard lost, but also that the cladding was changed from concrete to steel, a change for the better. It is one of the most impressive aspects of the project that within this reduced budget the architect has managed to maintain an intensity and integrity of detail and a sparse but carefully controlled palette of materials. This creative ingenuity extends to all the spaces of the building, from the drama of the galleries to the turntable display cabinets in the shop that allow a flexible use of space, the offices with their complementary storage and furniture, and even those undercroft plant areas.

The building can be enjoyed at the most accessible level of its formal resolutions and contrasts, like the vertiginous ascent of the tower and the cave-like exhibition settings, but it also allows a number of readings and metaphorical associations. This attitude to narrative is rare in contemporary architecture and sets a difficult agenda to pull off, particularly with the ambitious and provocative themes of war and museum. Le Corbusier called for an end to symbolism in buildings; here Libeskind has made a powerful case for the argument that they can have meaning beyond function.

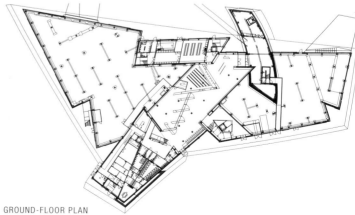

GROUND-FLOOR PLAN

KUNSTHAUS .GRAZ, AUSTRIA .PETER COOK AND COLIN FOURNIER

This is the architects' first building, but when you realize that one of them is in his sixties and has already won one of architecture's top prizes, the Royal Gold Medal, for his teaching and theory, then the quality of this blue amoeba with its roof covered in suckers is less surprising. Peter Cook was a leading light in Archigram, the group that inspired generations of architects with their radical ideas about buildings and cities. With fellow teacher Colin Fournier, he has finally realized some of those theories 40 years on.

You sense the importance of the Kunsthaus to Graz long before you have reached the city. The only pictures of Graz in the in-flight magazine show the blue blob nestling among prim red-tiled buildings. For a structure to be adopted so quickly as a symbol of a city and also to be loved suggests something special is going on. But as iconic as those photographs from the air are destined to become, the Kunsthaus is much more than a static object for aesthetic contemplation. It is a building that demands to be experienced and, crucially, moved through and around. The effect is visceral, sometimes shocking, but ultimately joyful.

It's known as 'The Friendly Alien', and a video by Viennese film-makers coop 99 shows it hovering over the city before nestling down in its new setting as if it belongs there. The Kunsthaus is surprisingly gentle to Graz and its inhabitants, yet people stand and stare, always with smiles on their faces. At night the curved façade is animated by a set of pulsing lights, softly spelling out words or displaying digital art.

Inside, the building is designed as a journey. The main galleries are raised up in the blue volume, with an open public area below directly connecting to the street. No pompous institutional threshold here, but a real openness and welcome, with reception area, lecture space and café spilling into one other. A sloping travelator drops down from above like a tongue, imparting a sense of drama and anticipation to the entering of the galleries.

It is here that you encounter the first shock: the toughness of the gallery

CLIENT KUNSTHAUS AG
LOCAL ARCHITECT ARCHITECKTUR CONSULT
STRUCTURAL ENGINEER BOLLINGER & GROHMANN, FRANKFURT
SERVICES ENGINEER HL – TECHNIK AG, MUNICH
LIGHTING DESIGN KRESS & ADAMS
ELECTRONIC DISPLAY REALITIES: UNITED
CONTRACTOR SFL GMBH
CONTRACT VALUE € 40 MILLION
COMPLETION DATE SEPTEMBER 2003
GROSS INTERNAL AREA 12,000 SQUARE METRES
PHOTOGRAPHERS KUNSTHAUS GRAZ/LMJ GRAZ/NIKI LACKNER (PAGES 29 AND 31)/EDUARDO MARTINEZ (PAGE 30)

interiors confounding the sensuous expectations generated by the exterior. Two raw slabs of concrete for floor and ceiling and the slightly curved exterior walls provide a robust, even uncompromising setting for art, a million miles from the habitual cool white box. This aspect of the design has been criticized by others, but this seems to miss the point. Art can and should be displayed in a variety of settings. The Kunsthaus exposes two fallacies implicitly perpetuated by its critics: first, that a white box is in some way a 'neutral' setting; second, that art should be set against a modernist background. The curators at the Kunsthaus are clear that the very toughness of the galleries presents not a problem but a creative challenge, forcing them to reconsider how best to display their temporary exhibitions.

Another travelator takes you up to the top gallery. Where the external image of those nozzles reaching skywards has set up an expectation of a sensual interior suffused with light bounced off the metallic mesh of the inner walls, as a result of budget cuts the upper space is dominated instead by spirals of fluorescent light coiling up the nozzles. From the top gallery you take the stairs up to the final level, the so-called 'Needle', a long glazed space, projecting precariously over the rooftops. This provides a welcome release back to the city after the intensity of the galleries.

The Kunsthaus works best as series of events. On the route down the quite normal concrete staircase, you are suddenly jolted by glimpses of the blueness against the old city fabric. This is not an architecture that should be judged against normal values of refinement or aesthetics; in a way its very bagginess is its most appealing and humane feature. The Kunsthaus transcends limits in providing a new architectural experience that welcomes engagement, enjoyment and exhilaration.

Architecture for fun, and why not?

GROUND-FLOOR PLAN

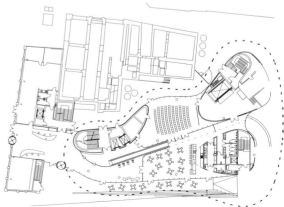

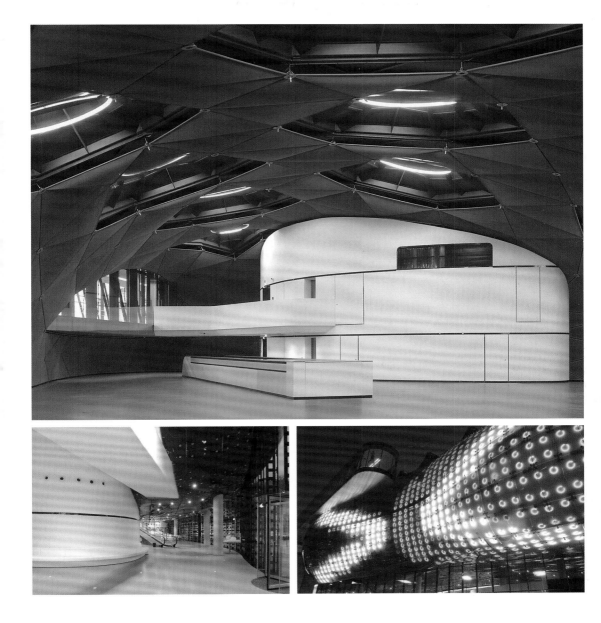

PHOENIX INITIATIVE
.COVENTRY .MACCORMAC JAMIESON PRICHARD

The *cause célèbre* of post-war city planning in the aftermath of the Blitz that destroyed its medieval cathedral, and a paradigm in the field of traffic segregation and pedestrianization, Coventry had fallen from grace in the last quarter of the twentieth century, and was in desperate need of some loving care and attention. It has got all that and more from MacCormac Jamieson Prichard and the design team, in the shape of an ambitious masterplan incorporating five new landscaped spaces, eight new collaborative public artworks, a visitors' interpretation centre, a mixed-use development comprising 84 apartments and 300 square metres of retail, accommodation for cathedral staff and a new entrance for the Coventry Motor Museum. All this had to work in the context of re-routing roads, providing full pedestrian (including disabled) access, and within the significant planning and conservation constraints of listed buildings, scheduled historical monuments, ancient remains and excavations.

A glance at the before-and-after drawings shows the skills that the designers have used in knitting together what was a fractured and neglected urban scene. At a time when so much urban regeneration is focused on the production of individual buildings, it is rare to come across a scheme that is as much about the spaces between them as it is about the buildings themselves. The result is one of the most impressive sequences of public spaces to have been created in the United Kingdom in recent memory. Already the marks of catalytic regeneration are evident, with developers moving in to the surrounding areas.

This thoughtful scheme successfully creates quality public open spaces from the formerly run-down Cathedral Quarter. Perhaps the single most impressive thing is that it does not rely on one key historical element, or one new intervention. The complex and sometimes conflicting requirements of the brief are revealed and integrated within an accessible and well-constructed civic environment of stone, steel, glass and water. The highlights – the scheme is bold enough to allow them without being overwhelmed by them – include Millennium Place with Françoise Schein's Time Zone Clock, Alex

CLIENT COVENTRY CITY COUNCIL
EXECUTIVE ARCHITECTS (PHASE II) PCPT ARCHITECTS
LANDSCAPE ARCHITECT AND URBAN DESIGNER RUMMEY DESIGN ASSOCIATES
ART CONSULTANT VIVIEN LOVELL – MODUS OPERANDI ART CONSULTANTS
ARTISTS SUSANNA HERON, CHRIS BROWNE, DAVID WARD, KATE WHITEFORD, FRANÇOISE SCHEIN, JOCHEN GERZ, ALEX BELESCHENKO, DAVID MORLEY
STRUCTURAL ENGINEERS BABTIE (HARRIS & SUTHERLAND)/DEWHURST MACFARLANE/WHITBYBIRD
SERVICES ENGINEER MICHAEL POPPER ASSOCIATES
LIGHTING DESIGNER SPEIRS & MAJOR ASSOCIATES
QS WT PARTNERSHIP
HIGHWAYS ENGINEER THE BABTIE GROUP
CONTRACTORS BALFOUR BEATTY/ BUTTERLEY CONSTRUCTION/ GALLIFORD TRY
CONTRACT VALUE £50 MILLION
COMPLETION DATE 2003
PHOTOGRAPHER MARK GOODWIN

COVENTRY ALSO SHORTLISTED FOR RIBA/ARTS COUNCIL ENGLAND CLIENT OF THE YEAR

Beleschenko's blue glass bridge and Susanna Heron's dramatic water feature in Priory Place. All these are held together in a sequence that is broadly chronological – moving down the hill from the medieval remains of the original priory to the modernity of Millennium Place. The view of the piazza is framed by the Whittle Arch, commemorating the local inventor of the jet engine. This is not an artwork, but appropriately architecture and engineering in equal part, and is the result of a sketch doodled by MacCormac during a meeting with the planners.

For the client, Chris Beck, this is the culmination of a lifetime's selfless work in public service. But the Phoenix Initiative is far more than the work of one man; it is testimony to the tremendous bravery of the city council as a whole in its commitment to spending on the public realm. Equally, it is not a profligate scheme: there is plenty of value engineering alongside the poetry. Beleschenko designed his footbridge with 22 different-shaped blue glass fins, each of which would have taken months to replace. At Beck's insistence, these were reduced to four shapes, with huge short- and long-term cost savings. To date only two have been broken – a sign of the respect Coventry people have for the initiative.

The collaboration involves more than a visionary risk-taking client and a sensitive and imaginative architect; it also involves a large number of artists and engineers. The considered integration of art, landscape and architecture, together with such issues as traffic engineering that are so often afterthoughts, provides a coherence that is a model for other local authorities to follow. In one move, a bold city council has used architecture and urban design not only to make better places, but also to put itself on the European map. It has taken such cities as Barcelona and Manchester to show that publicly led regeneration really does work; now the people of Coventry have something to be proud of once again. It has given them new heart and their city a new heart too.

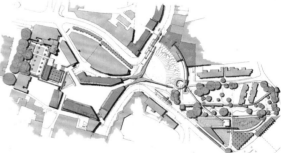

SITE PLAN

THE SPIRE
.DUBLIN, IRELAND .IAN RITCHIE ARCHITECTS

Locals call it 'the Spoike'. Dubliners were unsurprisingly sceptical when an Englishman won the competition to replace that imperial symbol, Nelson's Pillar, blown up by republicans in 1966. The date and location were significant: a British hero had been toppled on the exact site of the Easter 1916 Rebellion, 50 years on. This was terrorism as carefully orchestrated drama. But most people today, even Dublin's taxi drivers, have been won over by the simple beauty of Ian Ritchie's 120-metre-high stainless-steel spire. There are still plenty of jokes about it – a hypodermic monument to the druggies of north Dublin, etc. – but they tend to be good-humoured now. And people like the fact that it's more a memorial to the future than it is to the past. This, remarkably, is one of three (out of six) Stirling-shortlisted projects that have arisen from the wreckage of bombings (the Gherkin is on the site of the Baltic Exchange, bombed by the IRA, and Coventry was flattened by the German airforce).

In the 1960s Dublin was struggling economically, but by the 1990s when the competition was held to replace the pillar it was a different place. Ireland was undergoing the greatest economic boom in its history, and the whole city was being regenerated. Ireland's outlook, linked to the USA and the European Community, had changed beyond recognition. The entries to the competition ranged from the sublime to the plain bonkers. It was a foregone conclusion that the result would be the subject of national controversy.

The winning scheme means nothing in itself but it holds other forces in place. Its function is to charge the space around it. One critic described it as the apotheosis of boom-time modern Ireland: globalized, placeless and empty of cultural identity. To others it represents a new phase of confidence and optimism, an escape from the nightmare of history. It stands apart from the histrionics that are increasingly associated with buildings and public art dealing with memory, trauma and history. When it comes to politics and history in Ireland, Seamus Heaney advised, 'Whatever you say, say nothing'. The Spire does nothing with considerable skill.

CLIENT DUBLIN CITY COUNCIL
STRUCTURAL ENGINEER ARUP
SERVICES ENGINEER ARUP
QS DAVIS LANGDON
CONTRACTOR SIAC RADLEY JOINT VENTURE
CONTRACT VALUE £3.07 MILLION
COMPLETION DATE JULY 2003
GROSS INTERNAL AREA 7 SQUARE METRES
PHOTOGRAPHER BARRY MASON

It would be an easy but mistaken assumption to believe that the design of a 120-metre single object in an open urban context would be a simple matter. Nothing could be further from the truth, as this project demonstrates. Every single decision, from the diameter of the base to the materials used, the landscape context and the lighting regime, has required intense thought by both the architect and associated consultants. The result is a true icon for a European capital city, confident of itself and its ability to produce cultural statements of significance.

The Spire is first visible on the Dublin skyline as an object of extreme slenderness whose scale is impossible to guess. Once you know what you are looking at, the anticipation of seeing how this implausibly attenuated needle hits the ground begins to grow. When it is finally revealed along O'Connell Street the slenderness of the whole is remarkable, but in this context – set within the broad and newly landscaped street – the Spire takes on the identity of a civic monument – significant but not necessarily dominating its context.

If approached on the east–west axis, the effect is different again. Here the relatively narrow width and small scale of Henry and Talbot Streets with their tight bustle of people closely frames the Spire and it becomes a city landmark, terminating the vista and constantly changing in response to light and sky. To watch the constant flow of people brushing past the base of the Spire suggests that this technically (and politically) challenging project has swiftly been adopted by Dublin as a natural part of the city fabric.

This is also 'day-for-night' architecture, where the more celebratory side to this urban marker comes into play. The apparent effortlessness of the Spire belies the long and difficult business of bringing it into being.

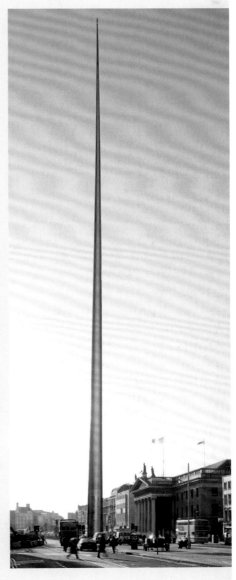

PLANS

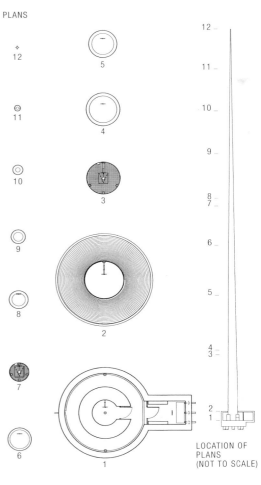

12
11
10
9
8
7
6

5
4
3
2
1

8
7

6

5

4
3

2
1

LOCATION OF
PLANS
(NOT TO SCALE)

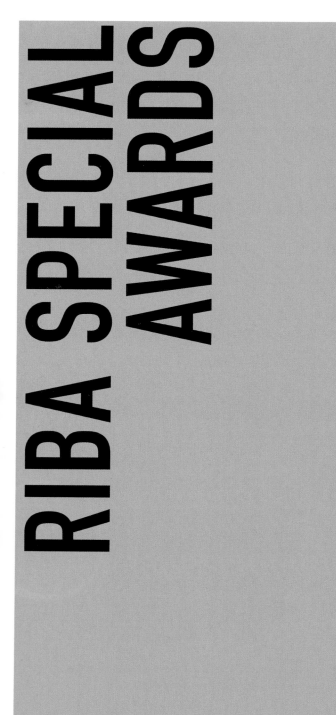

RIBA SPECIAL AWARDS

The RIBA Special Awards are chosen from RIBA Award winners. They are assessed by panels that include specialist judges in the various fields who pay further visits to the shortlisted buildings. These seven awards reflect the diversity of architecture and reward the wide variety of specialist skills involved in delivering good buildings.

THE ARCHITECTS' JOURNAL FIRST BUILDING AWARD

The Architects' Journal First Building Award, worth £5000, is given for an architect's first stand-alone building and is sponsored by *The Architects' Journal* with Robin Ellis Design and Construction. Previous winners have been Cedar House in Logiealmond by Walker Architecture, Barnhouse, Highgate, by Sutherland Hussey Architects and, last year, No. 1 Centaur Street, London SE1, by de Rijke Marsh Morgan.

The Architects' Journal, founded in 1895, is the premier paid-for UK architectural weekly. Robin Ellis Design and Construction, the award's co-sponsors, were responsible for key parts of the refurbishment of the RIBA's headquarters in Portland Place, London.

It takes courage for an architect to set up on their own after seven years of training, and often several more years spent in the relatively safe environment of a bigger practice. This award is for those who have made that break and proved they can do it on their own.

The award was judged by a panel comprising: Barrie Evans, buildings editor of *The Architects' Journal*, Robin Ellis of Robin Ellis Design Build, and Alex de Rijke of de Rijke Marsh Morgan, last year's winner. They visited:
THE BLACK HOUSE, PRICKWILLOW, BY MOLE ARCHITECTS; DOUBLE HOUSE, LONDON, BY WOOLF ARCHITECTS; AND IN-BETWEEN, LONDON, BY ANNALIE RICHES, SILVIA ULLMAYER AND BARTI GARIBALDO.

The winner was IN-BETWEEN.

IN-BETWEEN
.LONDON N16 .ANNALIE RICHES, SILVIA ULLMAYER AND BARTI GARIBALDO

This modest and ingenious development in a discreet corner of London brings a smile to the faces of all who see it. It is by two architects and a designer, who met during their diploma course at the University of North London (now London Metropolitan). Two years later they embarked on a communal project to design and build their own houses. Having found a backland site 'in-between' two rows of terraced houses, they were initially told by planners that a bungalow was the only suitable building type. It took a year to get planning consent, but they were helped by new government density guidelines that enabled them to achieve their ambition of reinterpreting the English terraced house. It took another year to raise the finance through a self-build mortgage. Then each of them took a year out to project-manage subcontractors and to work on the build, developing useful carpentry and plumbing skills in the process.

There is of course a cost penalty to designing a non-uniform terrace, but designers aren't going to go to all this trouble to end up with a standard house. The balance they struck was to build a very simple terrace volume with a reconstituted-timber frame, a technology that allows ready personalization within. The terrace is divided into three identical volumes – one house with workspace, one two-bedroom house and two studio flats – by structural studwork party walls, each with a 47-square-metre internal footprint. This framing allows the south wall of the terrace to be fully glazed using lightweight polycarbonate sheeting and glass. Insulation is variously recycled newspaper and sheep's wool. The roof is planted with sedum. The result is essentially symmetrical but, as with Georgian terraces especially, a uniform façade can conceal variety behind.

Having jointly designed the envelope, individual briefs as well as individual architectural preferences came into play. In fact the architects/clients/builders deliberately established idiosyncrasies peculiar to each unit that would express their own personalities. The playing through of this idea, with both charm and simplicity (combined with the constraints of a tight budget), has resulted in a delightful scheme. It is a reminder of the value of direct

CLIENTS ANNALIE RICHES, SILVIA ULLMAYER AND BARTI GARIBALDO
STRUCTURAL ENGINEER JAMES BIRDWOOD BTA
SERVICES ENGINEER CAMTEC
CONTRACTOR SELF-BUILD
CONTRACT VALUE £348,000
COMPLETION DATE NOVEMBER 2003
GROSS INTERNAL AREA 285 SQUARE METRES
PHOTOGRAPHER JULIAN CORNISH

ALSO SHORTLISTED FOR THE STEPHEN LAWRENCE PRIZE

architectural design – in contrast to the work of some architects who try too hard to be too clever with quotes, gambits and tricks.

In working out these briefs each house is in some ways strikingly different – in being single- or double-aspect, making circulation discreet or centre-stage, how much the timber frame is featured, choice of flooring materials and more. The dominant southerly orientation shapes all the layouts. The fact that the unit at the far end of the block is in the form of two flats demonstrates that it is still possible to provide amenable living space at very low cost in a new-build project.

The exaggerated grainy aesthetic of the reconstituted timber and the general lightness of the envelope give the building a certain graphic, even pictorial quality. These are by no means typical architects' houses – there are a number of rough edges and corners – but these are no ordinary architects, and their general sincerity, as well as their clear intelligence, shines through.

They have produced three different units within the uniform frame of a terrace, inventive, full of light in their more public spaces, eminently liveable, an implied criticism of the uniformity of conventional terraced housing. Almost a demonstration project, it risks a queue of student visits.

This terrace of innovation and delight was unanimously agreed to be the winner of *The Architects' Journal* First Building Award. The scheme is an expression of collaboration within tight constraints. The struggle has been worth it: low budget, but rich in terms of space, light, ambition and resolution. A sophisticated debut.

SOUTH ELEVATION

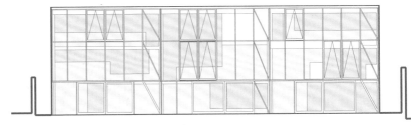

THE CROWN ESTATE CONSERVATION AWARD
SUPPORTED BY THE CROWN ESTATE

The Crown Estate Conservation Award is made to the architects of the best
work of conservation that demonstrates successful restoration and/or
adaptation of an architecturally significant building. It carries a prize of
£5000. Previous winners have included Peter Inskip and Peter Jenkins for the
Temple of Concord and Victory, Foster and Partners for The Reichstag and the
JC Decaux UK Headquarters, Rick Mather Architects for the Dulwich Picture
Gallery, Richard Murphy Architects with Simpson Brown Architects for the
Stirling Tolbooth and, last year, Newhailes House Conservation, Musselburgh,
by LDN Architects.

The Crown Estate manages a large and uniquely diverse portfolio of land and
buildings across the UK. One of its primary concerns is to make historic
buildings suitable to the needs of today's users.

The award was judged by Richard Griffiths, conservation architect; David
Pickles, senior architect in the conservation department of English Heritage;
Giles Worsley, architecture critic of the *The Daily Telegraph*; Roger Bright,
chief executive of The Crown Estate; and Tony Chapman, RIBA head of
awards. They visited:
MANCHESTER MUSEUM, MANCHESTER, BY IAN SIMPSON ARCHITECTS; SKER HOUSE, WALES,
BY DAVIES SUTTON ARCHITECTURE; COMPTON VERNEY MANSION, WARWICKSHIRE, BY STANTON
WILLIAMS WITH RODNEY MELVILLE AND PARTNERS; GRANGE PARK OPERA HOUSE,
NORTHINGTON, BY STUDIO E ARCHITECTS; AND THE KING'S LIBRARY AT THE BRITISH MUSEUM,
LONDON, BY HOK INTERNATIONAL.

The winner was THE KING'S LIBRARY AT THE BRITISH MUSEUM.

THE KING'S LIBRARY AT THE BRITISH MUSEUM .LONDON WC1 .HOK INTERNATIONAL

Built by Sir Robert Smirke between 1823 and 1827 to house the royal libraries of George II and George III, the King's Library was the first completed part of his grand design for the new building of the British Museum, and his finest interior. It was therefore an enormous challenge when the collection of books that gave the library its *raison d'être* moved out to the British Library and the room was left without a function. The challenge has been met brilliantly: the restoration of the room and its conversion to an exhibition about the history of the Enlightenment and the early collections of the museum itself have revealed it in its full glory as one of the finest in London. It is a worthy winner of the Crown Estate Conservation Award, reflecting the success of a skilled and dedicated team, HOK's Conservation and Cultural Heritage Group, working closely with the museum's own keepers and designers and outside specialist consultants and conservators.

The British Museum's project leader, Dr Andrew Burnett, declared at the initial design meeting, 'the room is to be the first exhibit'. Intervention in the historic fabric appears at first glance to be minimal, yet the more you look, the more you become aware of the work that has gone into the project. The ornate plasterwork of the coffered ceiling has been painstakingly repaired, the granite, alabaster, marble and scagliola wall surfaces cleaned by conservators, and cleaning of the floors carried out with hand- rather than machine-sanding in order to retain their patina. The original decorative scheme has been carefully researched by Dr Ian Bristow, later gilding overpainted, and a rather surprising primrose yellow painted on the circular and oval compartments of the ceiling to restore its original appearance.

The whole room has been invisibly serviced and beautifully lit, employing great ingenuity in using the hidden voids behind the bookcases and within Smirke's innovative fireproof cast-iron floor construction to run mechanical and electrical systems, including 200 kilometres of wiring.

The conversion of the library to house an exhibition of the Enlightenment is brilliant both in conception and in execution, and allows for the first time the

CLIENT TRUSTEES OF THE BRITISH MUSEUM
STRUCTURAL ENGINEER ALAN BAXTER & ASSOCIATES
SERVICES ENGINEER KLIMAAT CONSULTING
QS DAVIS LANGDON
CONTRACTOR MANSELL CONSTRUCTION SERVICES LTD
CONTRACT VALUE £5 MILLION
COMPLETION DATE DECEMBER 2003
GROSS INTERNAL AREA 1143 SQUARE METRES
PHOTOGRAPHER JAMES BRITTAIN

story of the museum and its early collections to be told. Seven themes, corresponding to the seven compartments of Smirke's interior, are illustrated by objects from the collections that made up the original museum, including geological specimens, stuffed birds and the wonders of nature (which later led to the establishment of the Geological and Natural History museums), as well as the emerging evidence of early civilizations through archaeological excavations, astronomical and scientific instruments, and much else.

These exhibits are displayed in the original bookcases, which were conveniently glazed in the 1850s, and in surviving and replica freestanding display cases. The cases are supplemented by pieces of marble sculpture and vases, carefully placed on new pedestals, reflecting the passion for classical antiquity, and the character of a gentleman's study, that would have been familiar to the early collectors.

In order to display objects in the bookcases, fibre-optic lighting has been subtly introduced, and the backs of the cases painted a suitably recessive dark red. The lighting has been carefully judged to allow all the objects to be seen clearly without it being apparent from a distance that they have been lit at all. Three thousand objects are displayed, as well as enough leather-bound volumes from the House of Commons library to convey an adequate sense that this is a library, increasing the museum's total number of objects on display by a staggering 10 per cent. There is something of interest for everyone, and the exhibition has proved very popular with visitors. At a time when museums are preoccupied with the problems of presentation, interpretation and accessibility, it is very refreshing to find an exhibition that allows the visitor to pursue his or her own interests within a very broad range, rather than one narrowly focused as in the new orthodoxy.

Impressive during the day, the King's Library becomes magical at night, the magnificent interior and the fascinating objects within it combining to make a scene of sheer beauty, stimulating to the imagination as well as to the senses.

THE MANSER MEDAL

All the RIBA Award-winning houses and major extensions in the UK were considered for this year's Manser Medal and four were shortlisted.

The Best of British Homes and *Planahome*, which publishes the longlist of the ten schemes considered for the medal, are published by Custom Publishing – now a part of Emap construct. Abrocour is a new company, partnering with BT, Intel and Microsoft to provide wireless internet fixtures and fittings and e-home applications to the residential property market.

The Manser Medal is awarded for the best one-off house designed by an architect in the UK. The award is judged by a panel including Michael Manser CBE, Past President of the RIBA; George Ferguson, RIBA President; Jamie Fobert, architect, winner of the 2003 Manser Medal; Michael Hanson of co-sponsors The Best of British Homes; David Birkbeck of Design for Homes; and Tony Chapman, RIBA head of awards. They visited:
WAKELINS, NEAR NEWMARKET, BY JAMES GORST ARCHITECTS; THE BLACK HOUSE, PRICKWILLOW, BY MOLE ARCHITECTS; BUTTERFLY HOUSE, DUNSFOLD, BY CHETWOOD ASSOCIATES; AND VISTA, DUNGENESS, BY SIMON CONDER ASSOCIATES.

The winner was THE BLACK HOUSE.

THE BLACK HOUSE
.PRICKWILLOW .MOLE ARCHITECTS

The three-storey Black House at Prickwillow is clad in Eternit pre-painted corrugated fibre-cement sheeting, similar to that used for many of the black-clad agricultural buildings of the Cambridgeshire Fens. Unusually, however, the cladding covers the roof of The Black House as well as its walls, the utilitarian material made more sophisticated by the addition of zinc flashings.

The barn-like quality of The Black House was a deliberate choice by Meredith Bowles, the architect who designed it as a home for his young family (two sons) with a study for his partner (the novelist Jill Dawson) and a drawing office for himself. They bought a small plot of land for £30,000 and built this five-bedroom eco house (two of whose bedrooms are used as workrooms) for £174,000. It took just four days to erect the lightweight timber-frame structure on concrete-piled foundations, which allowed the rest of the house to be completed in wind- and weather-tight working conditions by April 2003. The whole building programme took eight months from start to finish.

This one-off house is an exemplar to the house-building industry of how to design generous, low-cost, low-energy accommodation, where every square quarter metre of floor space justifies its cost. As a bonus it has magnificent views towards Ely Cathedral over the Fens, whose stringent scenery is complemented by the house's austere, ordered, but friendly appearance.

The house was handbuilt by the architect, so everything about it is calculated. It stands tall and proud in its flat landscape. Its model, the agricultural shed, in these wetlands has to be raised on stilts above floodwater to keep grain dry. So too is this house – sitting on a glulam ring beam supported by 10-metre brick piers – and it benefits in the same way from increased ventilation, obviating the need for damp-proofing.

This is a low-energy house but not in the tokenistic way of so many; here energy-saving is embodied throughout the design. Structure and cladding is all softwood timber, which the architect claims produces a net gain in oxygen because it absorbs CO_2 in growth. Most of the timber is recycled, as is all the

CLIENT PRIVATE
STRUCTURAL ENGINEER JJO ASSOCIATES
SERVICES ENGINEER MARTYN GAMBLE
CONTRACTOR MEREDITH BOWLES
CONTRACT VALUE £174,000
COMPLETION DATE APRIL 2003
GROSS INTERNAL AREA 150 SQUARE METRES
PHOTOGRAPHER RAY MAIN

ALSO SHORTLISTED FOR THE STEPHEN LAWRENCE PRIZE AND THE ARCHITECTS' JOURNAL FIRST BUILDING AWARD

insulation, in the form of newspapers. Heating is by a heat pump, which generates heat three times the value of the electrical input (currently wind-generated, but the system can be adapted to solar when the price of photovoltaics falls). The house is also well sealed. The windows are double-glazed with argon-filled cavities, and a low-emissivity coating on the glass reflects heat back into the house. The heat loss at −4 degrees Celsius is less than 5 kilowatts for the entire house.

But for all its eco-credentials this is also a very pleasant house to live in. It is arranged around a central kitchen lined in limewashed timber, with large west-facing windows looking out on to the fields that come right up to the house. A window seat encourages the use of the space for living and lounging, as well as for eating. External sunscreens fitted above the large ground-floor windows cut out overhead mid-afternoon sun in the summer.

There is a succinct quality to this building in a location lacking much architectural distinction – the two nearby Jonathan Ellis-Miller houses being honourable exceptions. You look at this one and think, 'Yes, just like that and no more'.

The Black House is a worthy winner of the Manser Medal 2004 because it has so many lessons for speculative housebuilders. To have built a five-bedroom family house of 150 square metres (1615 square feet) for only £174,000, excluding the cost of the site and professional fees, is impressive enough, but to have done so using prefabricated timber components with all their obvious advantages of precision and speed of construction, coupled with such a high level of energy conservation, resulting in remarkably low running costs and a comfortable living environment, make this a model of its kind. Most praiseworthy of all, however, is that the house has such a distinctive character, so different from its conventional neighbours and yet so appropriate to its rural location.

GROUND-FLOOR PLAN

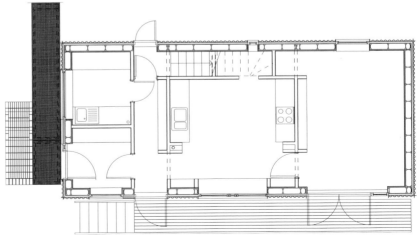

THE RIBA/ARTS COUNCIL ENGLAND CLIENT OF THE YEAR

The RIBA set up the Client of the Year Award seven years ago to honour the key role that a good client plays in the creation of fine architecture. Good architecture needs clients with both faith and vision. Arts Council England once again supported the award, as it has done from the start. The prize is £5000, to be spent on a contemporary work of art by an artist working in Britain. In this way the prize supports good architects and good artists.

Architecture is a team effort and previous winners have amply demonstrated that: Roland Paoletti, who received the first award for the new Jubilee line stations; the MCC for commissioning a series of fine buildings at Lord's; the Foreign and Commonwealth Office for a series of iconic embassies around the world; the Moledinar Park Housing Association Glasgow for their campus of buildings by a variety of Scottish architects; Urban Splash for their commitment both to design quality and the regeneration of Manchester and Liverpool; and, last year, the City of Manchester for transforming its public realm with a wide range of post-IRA-bomb projects.

This year's award was judged by members of the RIBA's Awards Group, which is chaired by architect Eric Parry and includes both lay members and architects. They considered clients of this year's RIBA Award-winning schemes but took into account a track record of previous successful commissioning, particularly where this has led to earlier RIBA Awards.

The 2004 shortlist was:
MAGGIE'S CENTRES for commissioning Frank Gehry, Richard Murphy, Zaha Hadid, Page and Park, Richard Rogers, Hawkins\Brown and Daniel Libeskind to design the Maggie's Cancer Caring Respite Centres; KIELDER PARTNERSHIP for the Minotaur, by Nick Coombe and Shona Kitchen, and the Belvedere, by Softroom; COVENTRY CITY COUNCIL for the Phoenix Initiative, by MacCormac Jamieson Prichard and a team of artists led by Vivien Lovell; SELFRIDGES, under the inspired guidance of Vittorio Radice, for commissioning a new store in Birmingham's Bull Ring by Future Systems, a new store in Manchester's Exchange Square and continual development at the London Oxford Street

location; THE PEABODY TRUST FOR its pioneering work in off-site construction, the realization of truly sustainable housing, and in particular its commissioning of this year's RIBA Award-winning Raines Court, London, by Allford Hall Monaghan Morris, and the RIBA Award-winning schemes at Murray Grove by Cartwright Pickard and BedZED by Bill Dunster Architects.

The winner was THE PEABODY TRUST, one of London's largest and oldest housing associations, as well as being a charity and community-regeneration agency. Founded in 1862 by George Peabody, an American philanthropist, the Peabody Trust Group owns or manages more than 19,000 properties across London, housing nearly 50,000 people. Its mission is to improve the quality of housing and life for residents, to tackle social exclusion and to build lasting, sustainable communities. It works with local communities, the Greater London Authority, local government and a range of voluntary-, private- and public-sector partners. Peabody boasts an award-winning track record and a reputation for quality and innovation throughout its social-housing development programme. By the time Lord Rogers's Urban Task Force issued its recommendations in 2000 – higher density, better urban design, use of brownfield sites, mixed use – the Trust was already delivering this vision.

Described by the RIBA as 'a pioneer of public housing prepared to spend money on design and energy-saving measures', the Peabody Trust has worked with many architects on numerous projects from small-scale infill to major regeneration. The threads linking this work are the ambition to set new standards in design and delivery and the commitment to employing good architects – some well known, others having their first major opportunity.

Three recent projects have been awarded RIBA Awards. BedZED, designed by Bill Dunster, incorporates numerous techniques to encourage sustainable, environmentally friendly construction and living. At Murray Grove, Cartwright Pickard used prefabricated steel units to create 30 new homes for rent. This work was taken forward by Allford Hall Monaghan Morris at Raines Court, the largest volumetric scheme for shared ownership built to date.

THE RIBA INCLUSIVE DESIGN AWARD
IN ASSOCIATION WITH THE CENTRE FOR ACCESSIBLE ENVIRONMENTS AND ALLGOOD

This new award celebrates inclusivity in building design and encapsulates an important new design philosophy. The principles of inclusive design can be articulated as follows: it places people at the heart of the design process; it acknowledges human diversity and difference; it offers choice where a single design solution cannot accommodate all users; it provides for flexibility in use; and it aims to provide buildings that are safe, convenient, equitable and enjoyable to use by everyone, regardless of ability, age or gender.

Winners of the ADAPT Trust Access Award are the Royal Academy of Dramatic Arts (RADA) in London, Dance Base, Edinburgh, and, last year, The Space, Dundee College, by Nicholl Russell Studios.

This year's award was judged by Sarah Langton-Lockton, chief executive of the Centre for Accessible Environments; Mike Hield, managing director of Allgood, the architectural ironmongers; and Tony Chapman, RIBA head of awards. They visited:
THE CHINESE ARTS CENTRE, MANCHESTER, BY OMI ARCHITECTS; CITY OF MANCHESTER STADIUM, BY ARUP ASSOCIATES; MANCHESTER MUSEUM, BY IAN SIMPSON ARCHITECTS; AND HORNIMAN MUSEUM, LONDON, BY ALLIES AND MORRISON.

The winner was CITY OF MANCHESTER STADIUM.

CITY OF MANCHESTER STADIUM
.MANCHESTER .ARUP ASSOCIATES

Inclusion by design is an aspiration that should inform the design process at every point. It is an evolving target – buildings that successively bear the imprint of the inclusive-design approach will over time demonstrate ever better ways of offering equality of opportunity and experience for all. The City of Manchester Stadium is an important milestone on the way.

This outstandingly beautiful arena, a totally designed, innovative and brilliantly organized modern football ground, started life as the main venue for the 2002 Commonwealth Games and is now home to Manchester City Football Club. Exemplary in relation to the consultation process and the involvement of users, this complex and beautifully planned stadium above all offers choice – of counter heights at its bars, in the multiplicity of WCs and baby-changing facilities, and in the seating arrangements. Seating for wheelchair users is integrated and is located in every price band and seating tier. There are, as would be expected, induction loops and an infrared system. Signage and architectural ironmongery are consistent and efficiently executed.

The circulation in, around and, all importantly, out of the stadium is managed with rare ease and generosity for everyone, successfully addressing the needs of large volumes of people arriving or leaving at the same time, be they able-bodied or disabled visitors, board members and their guests or the players themselves. In addition to the customary stairs and lifts, the eight spiral ramps provide efficient egress for those who can manage the gradient. In creating this design, a unique solution has been developed that provides an effective and safe dispersal system for all users. The use of the elegant ramped towers to support the cable-stayed roof props is typical of the co-ordination of structure, space and servicing throughout.

Historically, stadiums have been inhospitable places for many sectors of the community. The City of Manchester Stadium shows that the inclusive design philosophy and process, carried through into the management of a building and characterized also by ongoing dialogue with users, is the key to the making of buildings that are accessible to and usable by everyone.

CLIENT MANCHESTER CITY COUNCIL
STRUCTURAL ENGINEER ARUP
SERVICES ENGINEER ARUP
QS DAVIS LANGDON
CONTRACTOR LAING LTD
CONTRACT VALUE £110 MILLION
COMPLETION DATE JUNE 2003
GROSS INTERNAL AREA 50,000 SQUARE METRES
PHOTOGRAPHER DENNIS

ALSO ON STIRLING PRIZE MIDLIST

As part of the design process a series of seminars was held with disabled athletes and the Manchester City Football Club Disabled Supporters Association to ensure that the proposals were consistent with their needs. The success of the 2002 Commonwealth Games – the first in which events for disabled athletes were integrated into the main competition – and the subsequent popularity of the stadium with all of Manchester City's fans – most games are sold out despite the fact that capacity has been raised by 10,000 – both illustrate the success of the building as a truly inclusive venue.

At every level from overall concept to general detail it is considered and resolved in a way that no other recent British stadium has been. Automatic louvres in the corners and a transparent edge to the roof ensure the grass is always in perfect condition. The design allowed the Commonwealth Games' athletics track to be dug out and down a whole tier to allow seats to be sited near the pitch. Beyond the normal conference facilities and hospitality suites, the unusually comprehensive range of facilities includes indoor warm-up pitches for both teams and even a suite of police cells. These have never needed to be used; so far the fans' behaviour and their treatment of the building have been excellent.

While the stadium is the highly visible symbol of the regeneration of east Manchester, the city's vision of using sport as the motor for that regeneration is now being realized with both public and private investment. This project could not have happened without the vision and confidence of the city council both in bidding for the Commonwealth Games and in anticipating its reuse as a football stadium. Their understanding that such a development could provide the energy and funding for the regeneration of this, one of the country's most depressed areas, is exemplary.

GROUND-LEVEL PLAN

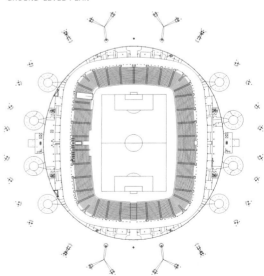

66 .THE RIBA INCLUSIVE DESIGN AWARD

THE RIBA SUSTAINABILITY AWARD
IN ASSOCIATION WITH SCHÜCO

This award is made to the building that demonstrates most elegantly and durably the principles of sustainable architecture.

The prize, previously sponsored by *The RIBA Journal*, was established in 2000 when the winner was Chetwood Associates' Sainsbury's at Greenwich. The other winners have been Michael Hopkins and Partners' Jubilee Campus, University of Nottingham; the Cardboard School, Westborough Primary School, Westcliff-on-Sea, by Cottrell + Vermeulen Architecture; and, last year, BedZED, London, by Bill Dunster Architects.

This award was judged by a panel of experts including Eric Parry, architect, chair of the RIBA Awards Group; Bill Gething of Feilden Clegg Bradley and chair of the RIBA's Sustainable Futures Committee; Bill Dunster, winner of the 2003 RIBA Journal Sustainability Award; and Tony Chapman, RIBA's head of awards. This is the only award for which the shortlist is not revisited; instead, the experts consider the environmental credentials of schemes as submitted by the architects.

The shortlist was BEAUFORT COURT, KINGS LANGLEY, BY STUDIO E ARCHITECTS; DAVIDSON BUILDING, LONDON, BY LIFSCHUTZ DAVIDSON; STOCK ORCHARD STREET, LONDON, BY SARAH WIGGLESWORTH ARCHITECTS; AND LIMERICK COUNTY HALL, LIMERICK, BY BUCHOLZ MCEVOY.

The winner was STOCK ORCHARD STREET.

STOCK ORCHARD STREET
.LONDON N7 .SARAH WIGGLESWORTH ARCHITECTS

Stock Orchard Street is an oasis created within one of the most hostile urban environments one could imagine, beside the busy rail approach to King's Cross station. The form, function and architectural expression of each element has responded to the site constraints at the same time as creating an original composition from a variety of low-cost materials: gabions of concrete rubble; straw bales; corrugated clear-plastic or steel sheeting; and sandbags (actually containing a dry cement mix). This is one of the few occasions where the constituent parts of many different low-impact buildings have been assembled to achieve an inspirational sequence of interior spaces. They transcend their original functional *raison d'être* and become architecture of the highest quality, at the same time as achieving low overall carbon emissions for buildings of this size and complexity. The judges felt that the lack of visible renewable-energy technology was more than compensated for by the live-work concept, and sound passive design strategies – and felt this approach shows how low-environmental-impact architecture can genuinely provide a higher quality of life and pioneer a fresh aesthetic.

This eccentric project, much discussed in the media, combines a wing of offices (for the architects) with a large domestic wing, through which pokes a five-storey library tower topped with look-out-cum-reading-room; all this set in a garden in which food is grown. The project is not only a pragmatic solution to immediate needs – somewhere to live and work – but also a research-led programme in which new ideas, materials and forms could be tried out.

The building, which featured in the first series of Channel 4's *Grand Designs*, can be seen as an experiment, an exercise or a series of gestures. A plethora of contemporary initiatives are contained within and without: green issues, sustainability, raw material, building with loose stones, straw, cement bags, recycled materials, avoidance of bourgeois elegance, avoidance of high finish, etc.

The architects are interested in the relationship between architecture and the

CLIENTS JEREMY TILL AND SARAH WIGGLESWORTH
STRUCTURAL ENGINEER PRICE & MYERS
ACOUSTIC CONSULTANTS PAUL GILLIERON ACOUSTIC DESIGN
PROJECT MANAGER MARTIN HUGHES
CONTRACTOR KOYA CONSTRUCTION
CONTRACT VALUE £635,000
COMPLETION DATE MARCH 2004
GROSS INTERNAL AREA 565 SQUARE METRES
PHOTOGRAPHER PAUL SMOOTHY

everyday. So the design is relaxed and playful enough to be able to accommodate the vicissitudes and the fun of everyday life. Most of the unusual techniques and materials are used not because they are novel but because they are cheap and accessible; what is novel is the idea of using them in this way and in this context. In the end the architects of Stock Orchard Street probably would claim not to care about elegance of composition or organization. And it works, of course. It is a big building and the living spaces are highly useable. Indeed, were it an old building it would best be described as rambling, and at certain times it does recall the atmosphere, and even the physiognomy, of a rambling manor farmhouse of the English tradition.

This is very much a work in progress: it took two years for the library tower to be fitted out, and a seemingly random first-floor projection is in fact the docking station for a yet-to-be-realized mobile guestpod to be parked across the garden when not in use. This is a house full of ideas, full of experiment and full of magic. The environmental-design approach was not generally driven by quantitative calculation but evolved as much through considered instinct as through strict rules. What has surprised – and silenced – its earlier critics is its practicality and its remarkable performance-in-use figures, which the architects only got round to producing for this award, when it was possible to provide not forecasts of energy use but statistics based on two years of occupation. The polemic impact of the design was equally important in that it aimed to raise the level of the debate about sustainability. Judging by the positive press coverage it has certainly succeeded in this aim.

This scheme represents a challenge to the classical or modernist strictures on language or consistency perhaps. But it is most important as an initiative that challenges the complacency of programme and manners of most London buildings.

GROUND-FLOOR PLAN

NORTH

THE STEPHEN LAWRENCE PRIZE
IN ASSOCIATION WITH THE MARCO GOLDSCHMIED FOUNDATION

The Stephen Lawrence Prize is sponsored by the Marco Goldschmied
Foundation. It commemorates the teenager who was just setting out on the
road to becoming an architect when he was murdered in 1993. It rewards the
best examples of projects with a construction budget of less than £350,000.
In addition to the £5000 prize money, Marco Goldschmied puts up an
additional £5000 to fund the Stephen Lawrence Scholarship at the
Architectural Association.

The Stephen Lawrence Prize was set up in 1998 to draw attention to the
Stephen Lawrence Trust, which assists young black students to study
architecture, and to reward smaller projects and the creativity required when
architects are working with low budgets.

The award was judged by architect Marco Goldschmied, Doreen Lawrence
OBE, and journalist David Taylor. They visited:
THE BLACK HOUSE, PRICKWILLOW, BY MOLE ARCHITECTS; LA CONCHA, VALE, GUERNSEY, BY
MOOARC; VISTA, DUNGENESS, BY SIMON CONDER ASSOCIATES; AND IN-BETWEEN, LONDON,
BY ANNALIE RICHES, SILVIA ULLMAYER AND BARTI GARIBALDO.

The winner was VISTA.

VISTA
.DUNGENESS .SIMON CONDER ASSOCIATES

Vista is a beach retreat in Dungeness that has been designed with wit, style and a great deal of technical skill and ability. The project was built for two London dwellers – one an actress, the other a lawyer – who need to relax over long weekends by the sea. It sits in a bleak environment close to the late filmmaker Derek Jarman's famous house and garden, and near the nuclear power station. It was orientated away from the latter building but carefully planned to let its owners wallow in views of the sea and the stunning beach landscape, not least when wallowing in the bath.

Dungeness is a planner's nightmare: historically a planning-free zone where squatter-built improvised houses dot the shingle. The scheme takes advantage of this freedom and develops the tradition in a way that responds to the drama and harshness of the landscape. The property was originally built in the 1930s as a fishing hut, and had been the object of countless changes and extensions. Now the architect (undoubtedly the first involved in the property) has stripped it back to its timber frame and extended it to the south and east, capturing fresh, eponymous vistas.

This delightful, tactile house makes extensive use of timber and plywood, and is clad unusually in a skin that is akin to the black rubber used in wetsuits. This, the architect explains, is a tremendous material that is both waterproof and 'breathable', and its black colour echoes the local tradition of fishermen's shacks, their timber painted with pitch to keep out the formidable elements. The detailing is meticulous and the architect has taken care to relate the whole building to its siting on the coast.

The house is simple, elegant and well planned. The living areas flow seamlessly through fold-back glazed doors out on to the sun deck, thus bringing the internal and external environments together. A 'snug' living-room has a well-detailed fireplace and even accommodates a baby grand piano. The walls, floor and ceilings are clad throughout in ply, as are the kitchen units. This uniformity of finishes is economical and functional, while being warm and elegant, raising the ante from beach hut to architecture.

CLIENTS PRIVATE
STRUCTURAL ENGINEER KLC CONSULTING ENGINEERS
CONTRACTOR CHARLIER CONSTRUCTION LTD
CONTRACT VALUE £112,400
COMPLETION DATE NOVEMBER 2003
GROSS INTERNAL AREA 92 SQUARE METRES
PHOTOGRAPHER CHRIS GASCOIGNE

ALSO SHORTLISTED FOR THE MANSER MEDAL

Remarkably, the entire 92-square-metre project was completed for just £112,000, well within the budget of £350,000 stipulated in the criteria for the Stephen Lawrence Prize. The original building on the site, now demolished, cost £55,000 five years ago.

There is a delightful but carefully controlled wit about the house. The cantilevered bathroom box contains the bath with a perfectly positioned corner window. This is set at head level for the bather, who can enjoy relaxing, uninterrupted views of the sea. Even the flush-detailed letterbox is concealed in the black rubber external skin. Clearly there was a symbiotic relationship between the client and architect in realizing this dream holiday home. (Visitors are obliged to stay in the 1954 Airstream caravan parked next door – itself not a bad deal.)

This is an understated gem of a building akin to a jewellery box. The RIBA Awards jury all left smiling. The Stephen Lawrence Prize judges decided that the scheme shows great wit in elements such as the entrance, where Conder has used an old shed to act as a foyer and humorous reference to the previous building on the site. But it also displays a keen technical ability in the execution of the fold-back glazed sliding doors and 'genius' in the way in which each element has been thought through and put together. As Marco Goldschmied concludes: 'One of the points of genius is that he has found a way of making it extraordinary and ordinary at the same time.'

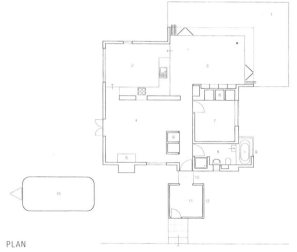

PLAN

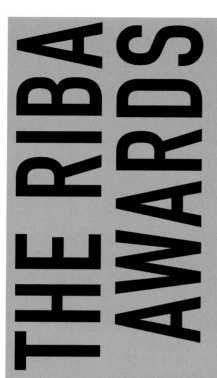

THE RIBA AWARDS

The RIBA Awards were established in 1966 and, until the creation of the Stirling Prize in 1996, were made up of national and regional awards. Since then all the awards have been national but they are still judged by regional juries. They are first considered by a regional panel (and visited if there is any doubt as to whether they should progress further); the resulting shortlist is then visited by the regional jury, including an architect from the region, one from elsewhere and a 'lay' juror – engineer, client, contractor, journalist, etc. The chairs of the fourteen regional juries then make their case for awards to the Awards Group (the scheme's advisory panel), which has the right to challenge their recommendations – and to query the ones they visited but did not recommend. If there is no agreement, members of the Awards Group have to pay another, what could be a third visit. And, still true to the principle that no project is rejected by people who have not seen them, they have the final say. The 60–70 confirmed awards are announced and celebrated at a dinner in June. From these winners, the shortlists for the Stirling Prize and all the other special awards are selected.

CLAVIUS BUILDING, ST ALOYSIUS COLLEGE .GLASGOW .ELDER & CANNON

The Clavius Building forms the second phase of a masterplan. It provides a new maths, science and technology block for St Aloysius's Upper School, with 25 specialist classrooms and related facilities.

Like the Junior School, completed in 1998 and itself the recipient of an RIBA award, this building sits on a very tight sloping site within a conservation area, close to the Mackintosh School of Art and Sauchiehall Street, opposite the main college and abutting a long block of tenements on Hill Street. To maximize teaching accommodation, a five-storey classroom block, reflecting the surrounding tenements, has been dug into the slope to provide an extra storey.

Although the brief called for traditional classrooms, the client also wanted them to be light and airy. The architects have responded by arranging them simply around a double volume that is as much about creating spaces for socializing as it is about circulation. They are refreshingly unlike classrooms, glazed to both the street and the social spaces rather than the enclosed private places of precedent. They are also visually linked with the other school buildings. From the street one can watch the teaching going on.

To the south the scale of the building changes so as to meet the School of Art. As it steps down the hill the section changes, allowing for social spaces and a garden area. The concrete-framed building's mass is well mannered. The quality of detailing and material is exemplary, with alternate slashes of glazing and concrete making for a vibrant streetscape.

The close involvement of the college at each stage of design development has ensured that the building supports its educational ethos and offers a stimulating environment for learning.

CLIENT ST ALOYSIUS COLLEGE
STRUCTURAL ENGINEER SIDEY ASSOCIATES
SERVICES ENGINEER HAWTHORNE BOYLE PARTNERSHIP
QS ROSS & MORTON SURVEYORS
CONTRACTOR MELVILLE DUNDAS
CONTRACT VALUE £3 MILLION
COMPLETION DATE AUGUST 2002
GROSS INTERNAL AREA 2500 SQUARE METRES
PHOTOGRAPHER KEITH HUNTER

GROUND-
FLOOR PLAN

DICK PLACE
.EDINBURGH .ANDREW DOOLAN

The remodelling of Dick Place is the product of a remarkable, and perhaps unique, trust between client and architect – which is perhaps as well as they were to have been married. Sadly this was not to be; Andrew Doolan died suddenly in the week the judges made their unanimous recommendation of an award.

The upper part of a largely glazed extension to a grand Victorian house, just visible above a garden wall from the street, offers only a hint of what lies beyond. An electronic sliding gate gives access to the garden, which has been entirely excavated to form a shallow concrete-enclosed pool. The route continues along the side of the pool, culminating in a three-dimensional crystalline structure that is in part a new entrance, part poolside terrace. It also encloses a stair to the reconfigured apartment that occupies the upper floors of the house.

The whole is an experimental fantasy in light and water. Everything is considered: the detail of the entrance door; the polished stainless-steel portal frame; the enormous sliding screen, which, when open, creates a sense of ambiguity between inside and out; the details of the kitchen and its relationship to the roof terrace sitting on top of the glass-scape. There are no raw edges. The exquisite detailing is sublimated to the composition. The extension of the architectural language into the original house is also well considered.

In the words of the lay assessor, 'This is a shimmering object of desire'. In taking on a rare private job, Doolan insisted that the client vacate the house to allow him to get on with the job and that he be allowed to refurnish the house, sending all the existing furniture to Oxfam. Both conditions were granted and the result is a stunning memorial.

CLIENT PRIVATE
STRUCTURAL ENGINEER JOHN BRENNAN
QS COLIN REYNOLDS
CONTRACTOR KANTEL CONSTRUCTION LTD
CONTRACT VALUE £300,000
COMPLETION DATE JULY 2003
GROSS INTERNAL AREA 2500 SQUARE METRES
PHOTOGRAPHER KEITH HUNTER

MAGGIE'S CANCER CARING RESPITE CENTRE, NINEWELL'S HOSPITAL
.DUNDEE .FRANK GEHRY WITH JAMES F STEPHEN

This beautifully put-together centre sits, seemingly isolated, high up overlooking the Tay Estuary. Looking out from the tower of this, the latest in a series of Maggie's Centres commissioned by Charles Jencks, even the most troubled cancer patient may be calmed. Its configuration unashamedly acknowledges this function and, although the entrance is at the hospital side, it largely turns its back on the hospital buildings.

The respite centres allow cancer sufferers and their families to drop in for information, counselling and emotional support, and for relaxation classes, but not for treatment.

The external form of the building features the stainless-steel-clad undulating roof, beneath which are the reception, relaxation room and dining/kitchen area. The tower contains a library, above which is a contemplative space with impressive views over the river.

The pervasive roof, which is internally an expressive skeletal structure of plywood and pine, represents extraordinary craftsmanship. It renders the whole with richness and a human quality. It does, however, pose challenges in its relationship with aspects of the orthogonal planning beneath. Nevertheless, it forms an 'umbrella' to a hierarchy of well-conceived spaces. The feel of the building is domestic: spaces flow from one to another in a relaxed and relaxing way. This organic theme is carried through in the architect-designed furniture: the sculptural cardboard chairs in the library and relaxation rooms, the curvilinear kitchen chairs, and the coffee tables and kitchen table designed to encourage group activity.

It is a mercifully far cry from what Charles Jencks has described as 'the trauma of hospital architecture', and a worthy tribute to his wife, who died of cancer in 1995. In her essay 'A view from the front line', Maggie Jencks wrote, 'Cancer does kill of course – but fear compounded by ignorance and false knowledge is a paralysing attack in its own right. ... Above all what matters is not to lose the joy of living in the fear of dying.'

CLIENT MAGGIE'S CANCER CARING RESPITE CENTRE
STRUCTURAL ENGINEER ARUP SCOTLAND
QS BURCHELL & PARTNERS
CONTRACTOR HBG CONSTRUCTION SCOTLAND LTD
CONTRACT VALUE £1.3 MILLION
COMPLETION DATE SEPTEMBER 2003
GROSS INTERNAL AREA 250 SQUARE METRES
PHOTOGRAPHER FRED STEPHEN

ON STIRLING PRIZE MIDLIST.
MAGGIE'S CANCER CARING RESPITE CENTRE SHORTLISTED FOR RIBA/ARTS COUNCIL ENGLAND CLIENT OF THE YEAR

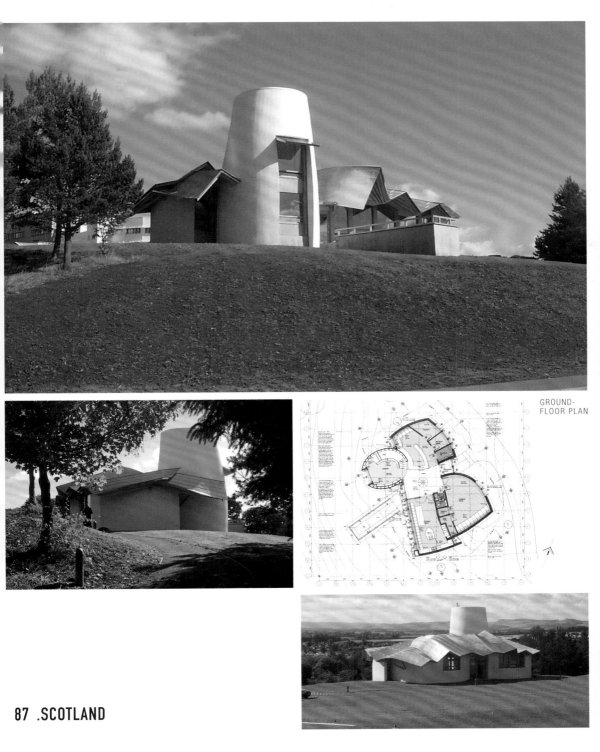

GROUND-
FLOOR PLAN

87 .SCOTLAND

THE BATIK BUILDING, BATIK CREATIVE DESIGN STORE, THE GASWORKS
.BELFAST .TWENTY TWO OVER SEVEN

The Batik Building provides flagship showroom accommodation for a leading contemporary design company and is the larger of two connected and clearly related buildings occupying a linear site adjacent to an arterial route to Belfast city centre. It is fronted by a curiously fenced yet open-format landscaped plot and enclosed to the rear by the perimeter wall to the former gasworks site of which it is part and from which it clearly draws inspiration.

The industrial feel is evident in the form of the building with its dominant pitched roof and truncated lantern, in the treatment of the elevation and in the controlled use of a limited palette of materials. Detailing is clean, bespoke, robust, crisp and pragmatic – stone splashbacks and cills together with inventive means of rainwater collection, for example, contribute to a building that displays honesty and integrity in its form and expression. The understated approach nevertheless provides an appropriately stimulating setting for the powerhouse of creative energy and activity within.

The two lower floorplates provide a dignified and restrained backdrop to the frequently changing display. Vertical movement and visual links between the two levels are enhanced and celebrated by simple but robust handling and an almost sculptural use of the materials forming landings, staircases, handrails and balustrades. The top floor displays an austerity of form appropriate to its use as a space for thought and deliberation while all support accommodation is grouped discretely to one end of each floor, adjacent to the circulation core.

High standards of workmanship combine with rigorous clarity of thought and result in a building that is elegant, fit for its purpose and a testament to the ambition and commitment of all involved.

CLIENTS BATIK INTERIORS/ORMEAU GASWORKS LTD
STRUCTURAL ENGINEER WM SHAW ASSOCIATES
SERVICES ENGINEER WILLIAMS & SHAW
QS BAILIE CONNOR
CONTRACTOR FELIX O'HARE
CONTRACT VALUE £795,000
COMPLETION DATE JUNE 2003
GROSS INTERNAL AREA 1115 SQUARE METRES
PHOTOGRAPHER GRID

89 .NORTHERN IRELAND

BERNERS POOL
.GRANGE-OVER-SANDS .HODDER ASSOCIATES

This is an exquisite community swimming pool on a spectacular site overlooking the wide estuary into Morecambe Bay. The site was identified by the local authority and an active group of enthusiasts who formed themselves into the Cartmel Peninsula Recreational Trust. Funding by Sport England had to be matched by the trust and 800 residents; the trust now runs the pool. The building is hugely popular and enjoyable.

Set below the coast road, the building is compactly organized on three levels with the changing-rooms, pools and café on the main entrance level. The main pool beyond the toddlers' pool appears to extend into the estuary through a fully glazed east elevation opening on to a terrace. At the lower level the fitness centre also opens on to its generous terrace with a sandpit and sunbathing area overlooking the valley. Wherever you are in the building, whether in among the excitement of the pool or the mental relaxation of the gym, the eye can stray out to the calm beyond, be it the sea in front of you or the woodland to one side.

The ancillary accommodation sits to the north side of the pool, looking both into the pool and on to its terrace. The side gallery doubles as seating for spectators and as an extension to the café overlooking the pool to which it can be opened up when needed. During the judges' visit it was full of parents and other relatives watching a children's session. Disabled access to the pool is via a much-used hoist. The natural light from the continuous clerestory and the east window wall is beautiful and provides good illumination with little apparent glare. Even on a damp, dull day the building creates a sense of joy.

This is a carefully built, classic modern building and a credit to all who designed, built and manage it.

CLIENT CARTMEL PENINSULA RECREATIONAL TRUST
STRUCTURAL ENGINEER ARUP
SERVICES ENGINEER ARUP
QS DAVIS LANGDON
CONTRACTOR THOMAS ARMSTRONG (CONSTRUCTION) LTD
CONTRACT VALUE £3 MILLION
COMPLETION DATE APRIL 2003
GROSS INTERNAL AREA 1594 SQUARE METRES
PHOTOGRAPHER MARTINE HAMILTON KNIGHT

CHINESE ARTS CENTRE
.MANCHESTER .OMI ARCHITECTS

This centre for the promotion and understanding of Chinese arts and artists is an exquisite insertion into a building on a street corner in Smithfield, inner north Manchester. The arts centre had been working as an agency for artists and exhibitions in other places but had no building of its own in which to hold exhibitions and to explain their mission. The brief developed with the architect involved many visits to other arts centres and much research; the architects have used every cubic inch to good effect with a carefully managed aesthetic that is at times both Chinese and Western without ever being kitsch.

On the street is the tea-house and shop with an entrance set back behind steel security screens with Chinese calligraphy cut into them. Visitors can be seen through elegant slots in the walls of the mezzanine internal office, providing security for no extra cost, and there are views through to the back gallery and out into the Smithfield courtyard formed by the walls of the old fishmarket. Appropriately, a minimalist fish tank is set into the wall of the office. On the ground floor is the resident-artist's studio and minute two-storey living accommodation, reached via a ladder (alternative arrangements are made for those unable to use the ladder).

The surprisingly large gallery is a real *tour de force*. It is a beautiful space with a high level of built-in spatial and service flexibility, all with a feel of the Orient. It even has direct loading access from a side street and opens up into the Smithfield Market for outside performances. Supervision of the gallery is provided through elegant slit windows from the office. In the basement a flexible education suite has its own out-of-hours entrance to allow both community and corporate use. All levels are economically linked with a platform lift.

Manchester is home to 30,000 people of Chinese descent and the centre is rapidly expanding its local network. Attendance at opening is up from 25 per cent to more than 50 per cent. The artist-in-residence scheme provides live action for passers-by, via a small window that still affords a degree of privacy.

CLIENT CHINESE ARTS CENTRE
STRUCTURAL ENGINEER HEALEY BROWN PARTNERSHIP
SERVICES ENGINEER HULLEY & KIRKWOOD
QS JOHN MAGNALL ASSOCIATES
CONTRACTOR MCGOFF + BYRNE LTD
CONTRACT VALUE £800,000
COMPLETION DATE NOVEMBER 2003
GROSS INTERNAL AREA 580 SQUARE METRES
PHOTOGRAPHER DENNIS GILBERT – VIEW

SHORTLISTED FOR THE RIBA INCLUSIVE DESIGN AWARD

HOYLE EARLY YEARS CENTRE .BURY .DSDHA

This is a radical transformation and significant expansion of two fairly inadequate nursery buildings, set back from the road in a depressed part of Bury, north of Manchester; domestic violence and drug abuse are commonplace in these parts.

The original nursery – the only one in Bury – was poorly funded and the victim of regular assaults. Through great determination, head teacher Clare Barker obtained funding to develop the site. She was totally involved in the design and, with the children, watched the construction daily from temporary accommodation across the road. Although she says 'it's been perfect', it was a constant battle to get exactly what she wanted.

The new building sits on the back of the pavement and is protected by a plinth of warm dressed dry-stone walling, moulded to the slope of the street. Thus the building protects the outside play areas from the mischievous or dangerous. The entrance hall is the head's favourite space and doubles as an assembly hall, looking into and through a tiny glazed court at the very heart of the building; it allows staff on reception to observe and control activity and feeds each group of children directly into their own spaces.

The building is full of light even on a dull rainy day. The interior design is controlled to allow the children's work to dominate and to provide the colour and stimulation. Careful placement of windows allows for views out at the right heights for children and adults. The nursery rooms provide the very necessary flexibility in use, and work well with the outside spaces, including a huge flat canopy for sheltered outside play.

The new building (little of the old remains) does not shout about its architectural ambitions but it is an exemplary project that works for the staff and children, all of whom are much less stressed than before. The school has a number of autistic children and the detailing takes their needs into account. One might say that this is working towards a new vernacular.

CLIENT HOYLE EARLY YEARS CENTRE
STRUCTURAL ENGINEER PRICE & MYERS
SERVICES ENGINEER ATELIER TEN
QS STOCKDALE
CONTRACTOR MCGOFF & BYRNE
CONTRACT VALUE £695,000
COMPLETION DATE OCTOBER 2003
GROSS INTERNAL AREA 410 SQUARE METRES
PHOTOGRAPHER MARTINE HAMILTON KNIGHT

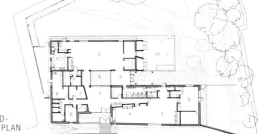

95 .NORTH-WEST

GROUND-
FLOOR PLAN

THE MANCHESTER MUSEUM, THE UNIVERSITY OF MANCHESTER
.MANCHESTER .IAN SIMPSON ARCHITECTS

This is an immensely complex project intended to turn a museum, which had since its foundation nominally acted as the public face of the University of Manchester, into a genuinely public and accessible resource. It brings together and reorganizes the circulation between the three museum buildings by the Waterhouse dynasty (Alfred's of 1885, Paul's of 1912 and Michael's of 1927) and two other university buildings. It does this by demolishing a fourth building, creating a new entrance court protected by the Oxford Road buildings and adding two elegant new pieces. Refurbishment is still in progress but the major structural work is complete.

It was previously very difficult to find your way around the museum and almost impossible in a wheelchair. But perhaps the biggest challenge was to make the museum intellectually accessible. The architect has worked closely with the museum's director and staff in making all parts of this intricate warren relatively straightforward to move through and has begun the process of making the right parts more accessible and the adjacencies more logical. The staff also benefit from the refurbishment: curators have been relocated near their collections and the below-ground connections between buildings mean that, at last, the museum really works.

The new entrance court behind the main Oxford Road buildings and the entrance hall in a new building work calmly and elegantly; the new cafeteria is accessible both from the hall and directly off Oxford Road, including out of hours. The new ground-floor education suite is easily accessible and flexible in use. The new parts and interventions, clad in lead and glass, are clearly new, allowing much greater sense of connection visually. The same demarcation is applied to the internal works.

The fire separation, environmental and electrical servicing, and lighting have been reorganized. The new staircases are continuous and consistent while dealing with the difficulties of linking buildings with different floor levels. Originally, the Waterhouse buildings had a clarity in themselves; in bringing them together the architects have pulled off an almost impossible job.

CLIENT THE UNIVERSITY OF MANCHESTER
STRUCTURAL ENGINEER FABER MAUNSELL
SERVICES ENGINEER OPERON
QS REX PROCTER & PARTNERS
CONTRACTOR M J GLEESON GROUP PLC
CONTRACT VALUE £21 MILLION
COMPLETION DATE JULY 2003
GROSS INTERNAL AREA 11,500 SQUARE METRES
PHOTOGRAPHER DANIEL HOPKINSON

SHORTLISTED FOR THE RIBA INCLUSIVE DESIGN AWARD AND THE CROWN ESTATE CONSERVATION AWARD

SECTION

1 PICCADILLY GARDENS
.MANCHESTER .ALLIES AND MORRISON

This is a brilliant speculative development in partnership with the city by a highly professional team – client, architects and constructors – who have worked together on other projects. In 1999 the city agreed that in order to pay for the redevelopment of the run-down square, to a masterplan by EDAW, they would sell off its Portland Street end to the Argent Group. Many of the doubts about this red-brick-framed rectangular block intruding into Piccadilly Gardens disappear on exploring the interiors of this quality building, which is punched through to allow views of the new square with its interactive fountains from Portland Street. Once this top-of-the-range office building with its ground-floor restaurants is occupied, the impact on this part of Manchester, half way between Piccadilly station and the business district, will be formidable and should trigger regeneration to the south and east.

As well as providing the top-up funding for the completion of the new gardens, the developer has acquired the empty Tadao Ando pavilion, a curved concrete structure with no clear previous function, and has let all three units. No. 1 Piccadilly Gardens has its entrance set in the pedestrian double-height gallery that cuts diagonally through into the gardens and beyond; this route is well used and helps to animate the square, as will the fully active ground floor.

The clients' and architects' experience have combined to make an extremely clever building. The 7.5 x 7.5-metre grid works at all levels in a deep-plan building with a partial central atrium to provide 2400-square-metre floorplates. The top two floors are set back and could be converted to residential use, with or without a restaurant.

Although fitted with fan-coil air-conditioning, the building meets the new Part L of the Building Regulations and has been designed to allow for the retro-fitting of chilled beams. Careful working with the specialist contractor managed to reduce the top-floor plant room substantially in order to provide additional lettable space.

CLIENT ARGENT GROUP
STRUCTURAL ENGINEER ARUP
SERVICES ENGINEER ARUP
QS FAITHFUL & GOULD
CONTRACTOR CARILLION BUILDING
CONTRACT VALUE £23 MILLION
COMPLETION DATE SEPTEMBER 2003
GROSS INTERNAL AREA 15,300 SQUARE METRES
PHOTOGRAPHER DENNIS GILBERT – VIEW

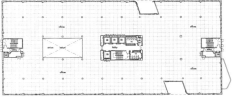

TYPICAL FLOOR PLAN

TFL INTERNATIONAL OFFICES
.RIVERSWAY, PRESTON .STUDIO BAAD

Spotting this extraordinary yet modest building in among the two-storey pitched-roof, brick-clad offices trying to look like houses, jumbled at the edge of a business park, takes your breath away. For the interior-design-and-build client, it provides stimulating naturally ventilated and largely naturally lit accommodation for staff, who have lost no time through illness since moving in. Just as importantly, the building works for the business by providing prospective clients with the necessary confidence to complete the contract.

The demanding client and the architect have collaborated over a long period and here they have worked closely to achieve a remarkable building for only £434 per square metre for the shell and core. The client built it and then fitted it out sympathetically.

The site was a contaminated former riverbed with possible methane generation. The building is a simple two-storey steel-framed box with blank end walls to the office floorplate. On the north, entrance side, beyond the methane-ventilation strip, the double-height top-lit slot atrium is faced with translucent Kallwall and allows cross-ventilation through vents in the continuous roof glazing. The Kallwall plane slides out beyond the building to make an entrance at each end, one for people and one for goods. These are locked shut at night by bold pink double-height hinged gates. On the south the fully glazed wall has elegantly detailed hit-and-miss sliding planes to provide light and air. They are protected by a 2-metre-deep zone faced with welded mesh screens that provide solar shading and security without blocking the view; the first-floor offices open out on to a mesh terrace within.

This is a remarkable essay in inventive architecture to provide enclosure with economy, a simple direct low-energy low-cost building with elegance – truly a delight.

CLIENT TFL INTERNATIONAL
STRUCTURAL ENGINEER BOOTH KING PARTNERSHIP
SERVICES ENGINEER REC MANCHESTER
QS WARRINGTON MARTIN
CONTRACTOR TFL INTERNATIONAL
CONTRACT VALUE £217,000
COMPLETION DATE NOVEMBER 2002
GROSS INTERNAL AREA 500 SQUARE METRES
PHOTOGRAPHER DANIEL HOPKINSON

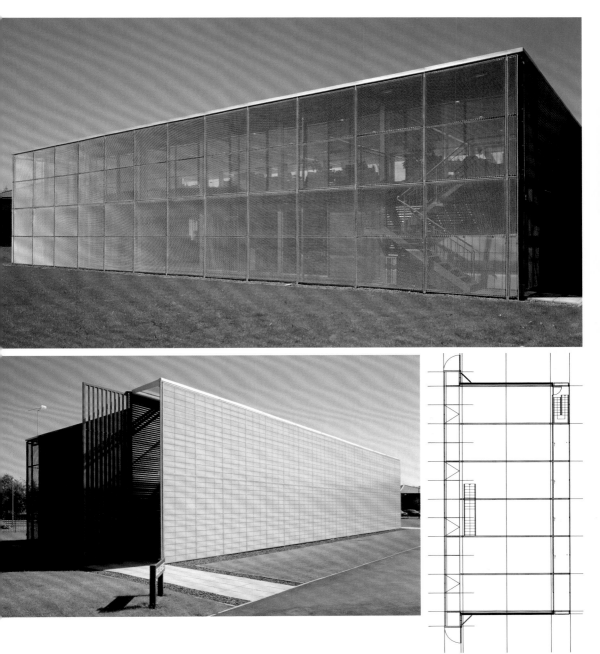

GROUND-FLOOR PLAN

THE MINOTAUR, KIELDER FOREST PARK VISITOR CENTRE
.KIELDER .NICK COOMBE AND SHONA KITCHEN

The choice of materials and construction methods are highly appropriate to the making of a modern maze. The broken blue basalt rocks enclosed in steel gabions have something of the quality of the foliage in a hedge maze. They make a solid enclosure, you can't see through them, but the gaps between the stones suggest a sense of permeability. The central chamber uses the same construction principle, but in this case the 'rocks' are pale-blue translucent glass, producing a surprising brightly glowing heart to the maze, even on a dark day. It lets the light in, but retains opacity and provides enclosure.

The maze is approached from above by a winding path so one has a clear overview of the whole construction, including the crystal inner chamber, before entering the puzzle. It looks small and simple from above but bigger and more complex as you approach and enter.

The judges admired in particular the precision of the walls; the achievement of a sense of discipline with random materials; the play on scale; the care taken in its conception and making; its relationship to the landscape and the surrounding buildings; and the rigour and clarity of the overall form in the landscape. They visited on a very wet and dark day, yet the stone walls reflected light on their top surfaces, and the crystal chamber at the centre of the maze glowed above the dark basalt.

There was evidently a close working relationship between client and architect: the client was very involved in the detailed development of the design and construction. This is very much an architect/artist collaboration. The Kielder Partnership is impressively committed to making art/architecture projects, and has a serious attitude to procurement – as demonstrated by the earlier project, the Kielder Belvedere by Softroom, winner of an RIBA Award and the Stephen Lawrence Prize.

CLIENT THE KIELDER PARTNERSHIP
STRUCTURAL ENGINEER ENGINEERS HRW
CONTRACTOR TK BUILDERS
CONTRACT VALUE £85,000
COMPLETION DATE JULY 2003
GROSS INTERNAL AREA 300 SQUARE METRES
PHOTOGRAPHER JAMES MORRIS

THE KIELDER PARTNERSHIP SHORTLISTED FOR
RIBA/ARTS COUNCIL ENGLAND CLIENT OF THE YEAR

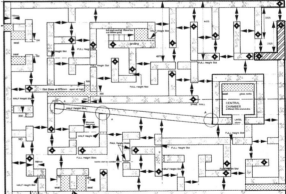

PLAN

SKER HOUSE
.BRIDGEND .DAVIES SUTTON ARCHITECTURE

This is a Grade I-listed building, described as one of the last great country houses to be rescued from ruin. It was in an extreme and accelerating state of dilapidation. The client, the Buildings at Risk Trust, showed extraordinary perseverance in fighting for more than ten years for its restoration, which began in 1999.

This part-Elizabethan building grew and was altered over generations and, given the extent of its ruin and the inevitable financial limits, interesting architectural choices about the form the building now takes had to be made. The result is rather wonderful. The building, now fresh with a brilliant yellow render, sits solidly in a bleak landscape.

The works were begun by an archaeologist, who carefully cleared the masonry from the collapsed south wing of the building. The stones were catalogued and stored so that part of the building could be reconstructed if adequate funds became available.

The rest of the house unfolds as a series of unique and extraordinary spaces. The great hall on the first floor displays the architectural approach to the works. The walls and ceiling are plainly plastered, but within this an ancient piece of graffiti is preserved. The floor is newly boarded but the fireplace was part of the house, with a replaced mantle. Stone window mullions have been carefully matched and a new timber screen added. A plaster frieze, which was probably installed in 1625, had disappeared, but when works began local people offered many of the missing pieces, which they had rescued from the crumbling house. Enough was found to reconstruct one side of the room, and the other three were made up from a mould taken from this. This whole ensemble makes an architecturally relaxed and satisfying room, with a comfortable balance of old and new. Equally interesting is the courtyard formed from the largely unrestored ruins, overlooked by a simple timber gallery at first-floor level. Throughout, the project has an architectural quality that lifts the spirit.

CLIENT BUILDINGS AT RISK TRUST
STRUCTURAL ENGINEERS EASTWOOD & PARTNERS/VERYARDS LTD
QS MILDRED HOWELLS & CO
CONTRACTORS DIMBYLOW CRUMP/ RESTRUCT LTD
CONTRACT VALUE £700,000
COMPLETION DATE AUGUST 2003
GROSS INTERNAL AREA 600 SQUARE METRES
PHOTOGRAPHER NEIL TURNER

SHORTLISTED FOR THE CROWN ESTATE CONSERVATION AWARD

105 .WALES

COMPTON VERNEY MANSION .WARWICKSHIRE .STANTON WILLIAMS WITH RODNEY MELVILLE AND PARTNERS

This is an extremely well-conceived, organized and executed scheme. The Grade I-listed house has undergone an extraordinarily thorough reconstruction and restoration, and carries with conviction the major and the more subtle interventions necessary for its role as a gallery of both historical and contemporary art, based on the collections of Peter Moores, son of the Littlewood's Pools founder, John Moores.

The buildings date back to medieval times and feature later work by Robert Adam, James Gibb and John Vanbrugh. The mansion is set in 16 hectares of parkland, much of it the work of 'Capability' Brown, between Stratford-upon-Avon and Warwick. Requisitioned during World War II, it was never inhabited again (though there had been plans to turn it into apartments) and was on English Heritage's buildings-at-risk register when it was taken over by the Peter Moores Foundation in the early 1990s.

Working with specialist conservation architects, the shell of the mansion has been restored to its former glory. Perhaps most impressive are the discreet nature of the complex servicing and the bold but similarly discrete additions: both the interior installation work and the two new buildings are as rich and refined as their predecessors. They engage well with the original buildings, setting up an interesting dialogue.

The new work – a two-storey gallery extension cut into the slope so it cannot be seen from the park, and a new education centre incorporating the front of a nineteenth-century brick coach house – has allowed the integrity of the original mansion to survive, even to be enhanced. The overlay of contemporary elements reveals and counterpoints architectural styles without favouring any particular period. The visitor experiences an unfolding sequence of mainly naturally lit galleries, from the restored eighteenth-century rooms on the ground floor to a series of more abstract and flexible rooms on the upper floors, where sliding panels can be used to obscure the light when conservation requirements demand it, as well as to provide a neutral backdrop for art.

CLIENT COMPTON VERNEY HOUSE TRUST
LANDSCAPE ARCHITECT COLVIN & MOGGRIDGE
STRUCTURAL ENGINEER GIFFORD & PARTNERS
SERVICES ENGINEERS OSCAR FABER/FABER MAUNSELL
QS DAVIS LANGDON (PHASE1)/JOHN AUSTIN & PARTNERS (PHASE 2)
TRAFFIC ENGINEERS W A FAIRHURST & PARTNERS
CONTRACTORS BOVIS CONSTRUCTION LTD (PHASE 1)/LINFORD GROUP (PHASE 2)
CONTRACT VALUE £17 MILLION
COMPLETION DATE DECEMBER 2003
GROSS INTERNAL AREA 4600 SQUARE METRES
PHOTOGRAPHER STANTON WILLIAMS

SHORTLISTED FOR THE CROWN ESTATE CONSERVATION AWARD

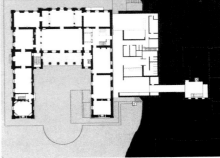

GROUND-FLOOR PLAN

THE MOAT, HEREFORD CATHEDRAL JUNIOR SCHOOL .HEREFORD .JAMIESON ASSOCIATES ARCHITECTS

The brief called for a solution to problems arising from housing the pre-prep classes of this independent school in a disparate collection of eighteenth- and nineteenth-century houses. The client wanted a contemporary building, despite the site being close to the cathedral and hedged in by listed buildings and even a scheduled ancient monument. The answer was a ground-hugging structure sited in the former sunken rose garden. Even then, inevitably, there were archaeological constraints, the site being that of the old castle defences.

The resulting building comprises nine small grass-roofed classrooms arranged simply along a usefully wide corridor. This includes services and features elegant and large frameless glazing as both roof and integrated marker stairwell entries. This modest linear building also seems to resolve effortlessly a number of level changes and planning issues with great panache and sensitivity. (This was achieved after an earlier planning refusal resulted in a better scheme.) The jury appreciated the clarity of the siting and massing strategy, something worked out between existing listed eighteenth-century follies and in relation to the surrounding nineteenth-century conservation area. The result treads a fine line between near invisibility and great presence.

The play area outside the classrooms represents an opportunity for future development, but internally the play of light and colour and the use of materials and the natural cross-ventilation strategy are already working well.

The private-education system, with its emphasis on tradition, is perhaps not likely to offer many challenges to the normal assumptions of education architecture. But this school should be congratulated for clearly briefing and then trusting its architect. It has gained a precise example of modern architecture, an asset to its complex of buildings, and, most importantly, an inspiring addition to the children's learning environment.

CLIENT TRUSTEES OF THE OLD HEREFORDIAN FUND
STRUCTURAL ENGINEER SHIRE CONSULTING
SERVICES ENGINEER ESDP
QS COMPLETE CONSTRUCTION
CONTRACTOR WHEATSTONE & PLANT LTD
CONTRACT VALUE £625,000
COMPLETION DATE APRIL 2003
PHOTOGRAPHER NICK MEERS

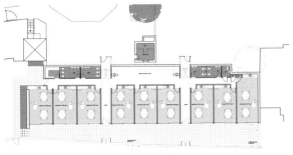

GROUND-FLOOR PLAN

109 .WEST MIDLANDS

SELFRIDGES
.BIRMINGHAM .FUTURE SYSTEMS

Future Systems have here not only reinterpreted the form and appearance of the department store, but they have also altered the role shopping plays in our society. Selfridges' proximity to St Martin's church, whose fabric has been restored and its function partially changed, may be coincidental, but it is not without significance. The shimmering blue and silver wave forms an ethereal and symbolic backdrop to the neo-gothic church. Clearly one of the most provocative buildings of the year because of its uncompromising and unprecedented appearance, perhaps as a consequence it is a project that has been somewhat overlooked or undervalued at other levels.

The client's demand for a new kind of department store has allowed the architects to develop a new typology. They have understood that conventional façades of windows are not needed and that this corresponds exactly with the more abstract logic of brand image. By inverting the stone-clad norm and manipulating form in three dimensions, they have produced extraordinary architecture within a regular construction programme and within budget.

But it is in the integration of the client's programme and the functionality of the interior that the building really comes into its own. This is coupled with a spatial dynamic that is more than a match for the decorative exterior. The interior is organized as a souk-like fashion marketplace, cleverly threaded together by circulation and daylight. Here is a brilliant manifestation of Jenny Holzer's observation that 'shopping is a feeling'.

That the scale of this conceptual-cum-practical approach works at the level of the Bullring urban-renewal programme is a more than a happy coincidence for Birmingham. The building is obviously as much a catalyst to local regeneration as it is a landmark – and a delight to use.

The bold and singular ambition of this building cannot properly be criticized as 'wilful' or 'not fitting into its context'. The problem is that the 'context' is also new, but has not risen to the opportunity anything like as spectacularly.

CLIENT SELFRIDGES & CO
STRUCTURAL AND FAÇADE ENGINEER ARUP
SERVICES ENGINEER ARUP
QS BOYDEN & CO
PROJECT MANAGER FAITHFUL & GOULD
CONTRACTOR LAING O'ROURKE
CONTRACT VALUE £60 MILLION
COMPLETION DATE SEPTEMBER 2003
GROSS INTERNAL AREA 25,000 SQUARE METRES
PHOTOGRAPHER FUTURE SYSTEMS

ALSO ON STIRLING PRIZE MIDLIST
SELFRIDGES SHORTLISTED FOR RIBA/ARTS COUNCIL ENGLAND CLIENT OF THE YEAR

PEN GREEN CENTRE
.CORBY .GREENHILL JENNER ARCHITECTS

A community centre for under-fives, Pen Green Centre offers care, education, play and inspiration to a deprived area of Corby. Given 'trailblazer' status in 1998 in the Government's Sure Start programme, the scheme provides drop-in facilities for children and their parents. The project was clearly the result of an understanding of how to extend and best use existing buildings, and a client with vision, determination and enthusiasm.

This is the kind of project that makes one realize just how rarely a building does much for the happiness and well-being of a community. The architecture appears relaxed and unaffected, but in fact richly rewards its users, who are (mostly) children, with a skilful and subtle combination of practicality and pleasure. A glazed cloister links new and existing accommodation around a central courtyard, which takes the form of a beach. In one corner is a delightful lookout tower, topped by a meteorological station. A new entrance and reception help to stitch together two old buildings and define a secure route in and out of the centre. The work is simple, but of good quality, thoughtfully detailed and constructed.

The jury was interested in the successful way in which the architects had fitted clients' needs within further 3D fantasies of the kind that are borne out of true collaboration. Beyond providing accommodation, the architecture was successful in offering sanctuary, and even opportunities for behaviour modification, to both adults and children. In no way patronising or institutional, it provides a world of internal security and external aspiration. For its lucky users it means a great deal more than just childcare.

CLIENT NORTHAMPTONSHIRE COUNTY COUNCIL – CHILDREN & FAMILIES SERVICE
STRUCTURAL ENGINEER WHITBYBIRD
SERVICES ENGINEER ENVIRONMENTAL ENGINEERING PARTNERSHIP
QS ROBINSON LOW FRANCIS
CONTRACTOR DEEJAK BUILDERS (RUSHDEN) LTD
CONTRACT VALUE £1.3 MILLION
COMPLETION DATE JULY 2002
PHOTOGRAPHER CHARLOTTE WOOD

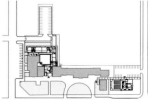

GROUND-FLOOR PLAN

SPARKENHOE THEATRE, SPARKENHOE COMMUNITY PRIMARY SCHOOL
.LEICESTER .ASH SAKULA ARCHITECTS

The client wanted to demolish a decrepit former dole office, housed in a 1950s prefab, and replace it with a new theatre building for the local primary school and its community. The diversity of this audience is demonstrated by the 40 languages spoken at the school. The architects argued successfully that the only way to produce an adequate theatre within budget was to reuse the existing building – and that it was also more sustainable. So the old building now acts as the entrance and houses services, adjacent to a new shed housing the auditorium.

Despite the lack of money, the ordinariness of the site and the off-the-shelf materials used, a bold and fascinating project has emerged. The complex of existing and new structures is clearly providing a good solution to the brief and, in an unusual way, is making sense of the budget, the location, and the vexing question of what constitutes sustainability, the logic of which often ignores the larger scale of recycling in the reuse of 'obsolete' buildings. As appropriate for the functions of theatre and for children's/community computer use, the interior has been prioritized, and is full of good ideas, simple, economical and fun.

The building's vulnerability to vandalism is clearly an issue but the client has no doubts about the design solution being appropriate to the area, and speaks warmly about how the building has already attracted local curiosity and new stakeholder involvement.

Generally the project demonstrates that a genuinely creative imagination in architecture does not always have to cost more to benefit directly and bring pleasure to clients. It has turned an unloved and unused eyesore into a vibrant centre of community life.

CLIENT LEICESTER CITY COUNCIL EDUCATION DEPARTMENT
ARTIST BHAJAN HUNJAN
QS AND PROJECT MANAGER CITY CONSULTANTS
CONTRACTOR ALLENBUILD LTD
CONTRACT VALUE £600,000
COMPLETION DATE JANUARY 2004
GROSS INTERNAL AREA 454 SQUARE METRES
PHOTOGRAPHER NICHOLAS KANE

ADVANCE DENTAL CLINIC
.CHELMSFORD .RICHARD MITZMAN ARCHITECTS

This is a real surprise: the ingenious insertion into an impossibly constrained site in an undistinguished suburb of Chelmsford of a skilfully designed dental surgery that is a pleasure to visit. The planners insisted on a pitched roof and the use of brick; the architect has subtly subverted their intention by giving them a monopitch roof and crisp brickwork with which even the Dutch would be pleased.

The plan is simple and logical and the design detail is precise and thoughtful. The layout is intrinsically ergonomically efficient and provides for the highest standards of cross-infection control, with patient circulation separated from that of staff by the surgeries. A storage wall that can be accessed from both sides houses all services, including waste bins, instruments and materials – an idea borrowed from American dental-surgery design but extremely rare in the UK. This separation of front-of-house and backstage activities helps to calm patients, as well improving hygiene standards. Lying in a dentist's chair looking at the blue sky and clouds through a carefully placed rooflight must soothe even the most frazzled nerves. It is an immensely restful and cheering interior achieved by an understanding of the basis of architectural light and form.

None of this is quite so surprising when one learns that the architect trained and practised for fourteen years as a dentist. This surely unique combination of skills and experience has produced a building that is completely in tune with the needs of its users. One waiting patient commented to the judges, 'I don't mind coming to the dentist these days'. High praise indeed. And it is working in economic terms, too, with more than 500 new patients taken on in the first year.

CLIENT DR ANDREW MOORE
STRUCTURAL ENGINEER DAVID BERLE
SERVICES ENGINEER MAIN GROUP SERVICES
QS HAMPTON
CONTRACTOR ZENON KACZMARCZYK BUILDING SERVICES
CONTRACT VALUE £320,000
COMPLETION DATE MAY 2003
GROSS INTERNAL AREA 142 SQUARE METRES
PHOTOGRAPHER NICHOLAS KANE

GROUND-FLOOR PLAN

BEAUFORT COURT ZERO EMISSIONS BUILDING .KINGS LANGLEY .STUDIO E ARCHITECTS

This project involved the conversion and reconstruction of a whimsical, pre-war Ovaltine chicken hatchery, to become the headquarters for a company devoted to the research and development of renewable-energy processes for the building industry.

Turning accommodation for chickens into that for people was never going to be easy, not least because planners seem to go easier on the former than the latter. Despite being in the greenbelt, the farm itself was not listed, but planning consent was nonetheless dependent on the existing buildings remaining unaltered externally. The courtyard was enclosed, and the horseshoe-shaped buildings had to be largely rebuilt. A new single-storey turf-roofed building incorporates the main entrance, linking the two sides of the horseshoe. Materials are either recycled from the farm buildings or are modern complementary materials chosen for their low embodied energy. No attempt was made to replicate the old Arts and Crafts style of architecture; instead, the new is unashamedly new, even if it has to be partially sunk into the ground and hidden behind banked earth and an array of photovoltaics.

It is, the architects believe, the first commercially developed building to be carbon neutral and entirely energy independent. It is served by every source of renewable energy, including a large freestanding windmill. What is even more commendable is that apart from the windmill, itself a design icon, the conversion and reconstruction has incorporated energy technology – with architectural style, minimalism, practicality and impeccable detailing – to such a degree that it is almost invisible. The project is a demonstration of how to absorb a technology that will increasingly become obligatory and an object lesson to the majority of architect eco-fundamentalists who incorporate such technology with the elegance of collapsed scaffolding.

CLIENT RENEWABLE ENERGY SYSTEMS
STRUCTURAL ENGINEER DEWHURST MACFARLANE AND PARTNERS
ENVIRONMENTAL AND BUILDING SERVICES ENGINEER MAX FORDHAM LLP
LANDSCAPE ARCHITECT CAMLIN LONSDALE
CONTRACTOR WILLMOTT DIXON CONSTRUCTION
CONTRACT VALUE £4.9 MILLION
COMPLETION DATE AUGUST 2003
GROSS INTERNAL AREA 2865 SQUARE METRES
PHOTOGRAPHER PETER MACKIVEN

SHORTLISTED FOR THE RIBA SUSTAINABILITY AWARD

GROUND-FLOOR PLAN

THE FORUM
.NORWICH .HOPKINS ARCHITECTS

This is a new city centre library, expanded to include a centre for community assembly, exhibitions, musical performances, BBC broadcasting, eating and drinking, as well as the serious reference and research activities of a library.

A disastrous fire in 1994 provided a rare opportunity for a new civic building in the heart of this historic city. There was also a millennium coming along so half the £63.5 million project cost (£25 million construction costs) was available from the Millennium Commission. Originally and grandiloquently called Bibliopolis, the inappropriately off-putting name for a welcoming public building was dropped during construction. The site is not easy, though, surrounded as it is by some of the county's finest buildings, including City Hall (1938), inspired by that of Oslo, and the Perpendicular church of St Peter Mancroft (built between 1430 and 1455), described by John Wesley as one of England's most beautiful parish churches.

The view of St Peter Mancroft inspired the Forum's design; the church is framed in the spectacular glazed end wall of the horseshoe-shaped building. Behind it is a splendid public arena where people meet for coffee and conversation or orientate themselves before using the other facilities. The wall of the library entrance hall overlooking this space is concave and also entirely of glass under a projecting roof that provides substantial shelter from rain. The rear wall of the horseshoe, abutting a busy city road, is of specially made brick, 19 mm longer than standard, perforated by smallish windows. The roof is supported by tubular-steel bowstring trusses, which form pointed ellipses, infilled either with glass or zinc. Below the building there is a large car park with direct access to all public areas.

It is an architectural *tour de force* and a major contribution to cultural and social life in Norwich. On the day of the jury's visit it was pulsating with people and their activities.

CLIENT THE FORUM TRUST LTD
STRUCTURAL ENGINEER WHITBYBIRD
SERVICES ENGINEER FABER MAUNSELL
QS TURNER & TOWNSEND
CONTRACTOR R G CARTER LTD
CONTRACT VALUE £25 MILLION
COMPLETION DATE 2003
GROSS INTERNAL AREA 20,000 SQUARE METRES
PHOTOGRAPHER PETER MACKIVEN

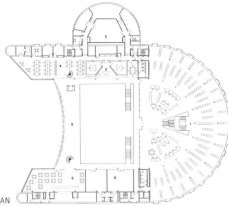

GROUND-FLOOR PLAN

WAKELINS
.WICKHAMBROOK .JAMES GORST ARCHITECTS

Set in a generous acreage of Suffolk landscape, Wakelins is a country estate on a small and manageable scale. A group of buildings, presumably once part of a smallholding, has been converted and extended to create an arcadian retreat and home.

The existing house, despite being Grade II listed, had been crudely extended and altered in the 1970s. Proposals to reveal the historic Tudor core and add a modern extension won support from English Heritage and the Ancient Monuments Society; less surprisingly there were a number of local objections. Nonetheless, planning and listed-building consents were granted at the end of 2001.

The main house has literally been reconstructed. The retained primary structural frame has been injected with so much fine oak joinery and other finishes that the new takes over the old to make a meticulously detailed and contemporary sequence of spaces, culminating in the new cubic volume of the extension. This inversion is unnerving, particularly when behind the veneer of pargetting and the slightly mannered glass in the leaded lights there is a feast of hi-tech gadgetry.

Compared with the painstaking restoration job, the new extension was simple. The latter-day timber-framed building went up in just five days. It is a rewarding surprise and plays well against the renovated building. The crisp skin of varnished oak boarding is a clever choice of hue, scale and material. A particularly well-judged and proportioned set of openings at different sizes and orientation mediates beautifully between the interior and exterior.

CLIENT PRIVATE
STRUCTURAL ENGINEER ANTHONY HUNT ASSOCIATES LTD
SERVICES ENGINEER CRAWT SIMPKINS PARTNERSHIP
QS SHERRIFF TIPLADY ASSOCIATES
CONTRACTOR VALIANT + SONS LTD, FA
CONTRACT VALUE £2.15 MILLION
COMPLETION DATE SEPTEMBER 2003
GROSS INTERNAL AREA 480 SQUARE METRES
PHOTOGRAPHER JAMES GORST

SHORTLISTED FOR THE MANSER MEDAL

GROUND-FLOOR PLAN

LIGHTHOUSE, POOLE'S CENTRE FOR THE ARTS
.POOLE .SHORT AND ASSOCIATES

As with so many good projects, success here lies in the process as much as in the result. Identification of the project's objectives, detailed briefing and cost modelling, and close co-operation between all the interested parties and the design team have helped to solve major problems of funding, programming and phasing, and produced a refurbished building that is popular with both client and user and is meeting the objectives of the business plan.

There were major constraints inherent in the building – a late-1970s arts centre the size of the Royal Festival Hall and the biggest complex of its kind outside London. The centre suffered from many of the problems shared by public buildings of its age: cramped foyers, noisy air-conditioning, tired and stained finishes both inside and out. Many of the best moves, such as creating the new flexible performance space and cinema, have resulted directly from these constraints and from the limited resources available; a £2 million reduction in Arts Council funding led to an intense but productive value-engineering exercise.

The major performance spaces have been improved technically in ways that provide greater comfort but that are not apparent to the user. By contrast, the front of house has been changed dramatically and rebranded. False ceilings have been removed to reveal the structure and services, and replaced by a hovering cloud installation and mirrors on the walls that distort the true nature of the space at level 2. This is not the comfortable illusion of a Victorian theatre. The ventilation tower on the façade is the new symbol, and owes nothing to tradition.

The entrance to the small lobby is nicely signalled by the projecting lift tower. Here the designers inherited a concrete-frame structure with large square columns. These dominate the foyer and first-floor bar but their mass is leavened by the clever use of graphics.

CLIENT POOLE ARTS TRUST LTD
STRUCTURAL ENGINEER SINCLAIR KNIGHT MERZ
SERVICES ENGINEER MAX FORDHAM LLP
QS NORTHCROFT
CONTRACTOR BLUESTONE PLC
CONTRACT VALUE £5.68 MILLION
COMPLETION DATE NOVEMBER 2003
PHOTOGRAPHER PETER COOK – VIEW

GRANGE PARK OPERA HOUSE
.NORTHINGTON .STUDIO E ARCHITECTS

Grange Park is the ruin of one of the earliest and finest Greek Revival houses in the country. It was created from an earlier building from 1804 onwards first by Wilkins, and then by Smirke and C R Cockerell. It was saved from demolition in 1972 and made safe as a roofed but windowless shell. Of the once fine interiors, more lath than plaster remains.

The conversion to its current use as a 'summer season only' opera house demonstrates an original approach to conservation and a well-worked adaptation. The main Wilkins temple and Cockerell orangery (once the largest in Europe) remain unrestored and their ruined state is celebrated rather than concealed. Users are protected from falling plaster by netting, and for two months opera-goers dine in the crumbling temple. In the shell of the conservatory, an elegant if eclectic horseshoe of unfinished plaster boxes (its form copied from an early Wilkins theatre) forms the auditorium. The new interventions in this space are self-consciously transient in feel (raw plaster, sawn-board flooring, strip lighting).

New stage and backstage areas are screened from the view of the house and from the landscaped park to the south by a new wall replacing that of the Smirke wing. The considerable height of the stage is kept below the existing orangery roofline by cutting the auditorium and stage into the ground and avoiding a fly tower. On the less prominent north and west sides the stage forms a simple oak-clad box (also weathering well to tone with the original render) on a brick and flint plinth. The scenery dock-link towards the temple is a plain rendered box, the sole touch of whimsy in the external treatment.

This modern intervention into a crumbling classic is handled with considerable style and wit. The philosophy behind the project poses interesting questions about how such landmarks should be preserved. While a scholastic restoration of the interiors would still be possible, one feels that this would lose the eccentric charm of this midsummer *jeu d'esprit*.

CLIENT GRANGE PARK OPERA
STRUCTURAL ENGINEER ARUP
CONTRACTOR R J SMITH AND CO
CONTRACT VALUE £1.97 MILLION
COMPLETION DATE SEPTEMBER 2003
GROSS INTERNAL AREA 1900 SQUARE METRES
PHOTOGRAPHER CLIVE BOURSNELL

SHORTLISTED FOR THE CROWN ESTATE CONSERVATION AWARD

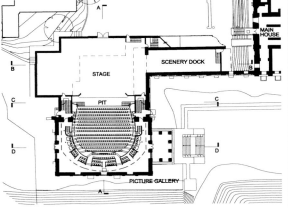

GROUND-FLOOR PLAN

MAIN HOUSE

SCENERY DOCK

STAGE

PIT

PICTURE GALLERY

A

A

B

B

C

C

D

D

OSBORNE SCHOOL
.WINCHESTER .HAMPSHIRE COUNTY COUNCIL ARCHITECTS

The new school building replaces one on the same campus and sits at the top of a steeply sloping 4-hectare site. The slope dictates a two-storey solution, which sets an unusual challenge for a school, particularly one dealing with special needs.

The low-key but clearly legible entrance brings the visitor straight into the main circulation spine from which the layout of the whole building is apparent: this is not a building in which visitors or users can get lost. The change in level (half up and half down from the entrance) is handled by a long top-lit ramp dominating the south end of the long linear plan.

The building is clearly arranged with all classrooms in two layers on the downhill side, central corridors on two levels and major spaces in a single layer on the uphill side. The only problem with this is the loss of light to the lower level and corridor and, to a lesser extent, classrooms. The double-height elliptical resources area breaks into the linear form above the centre point, reducing the unrelieved corridor length, while the lower corridor adjacent to the ramp is adequately lit through a glazed screen (etched with site photographs and architect's drawings). The lower-level classroom lighting is assisted by large sunpipes to the rear of the rooms.

The clarity of organization carries over into the rigorous, ordered and thoroughly competent detailing. Despite the totally glazed east-facing elevation, the balcony and *brise-soleils* control glare and solar gain, except for a localized problem on early winter mornings, dealt with by curtains.

This building works well at all levels, and is a very assured, thoroughly competent design. It does not break the mould, but stands out, in a field where we have come to expect a high level of quality in design, as a fine example of an established genre.

CLIENT HAMPSHIRE COUNTY COUNCIL
STRUCTURAL ENGINEER R J WATKINSON ASSOCIATES
SERVICES CONSULTANT CAPITA
QS HAMPSHIRE COUNTY COUNCIL
CONTRACTOR ROK LLEWELLYN
CONTRACT VALUE £5.9 MILLION
COMPLETION DATE SEPTEMBER 2003
GROSS INTERNAL AREA (SCHOOL) 3646 SQUARE METRES
PHOTOGRAPHER DAN KEELER

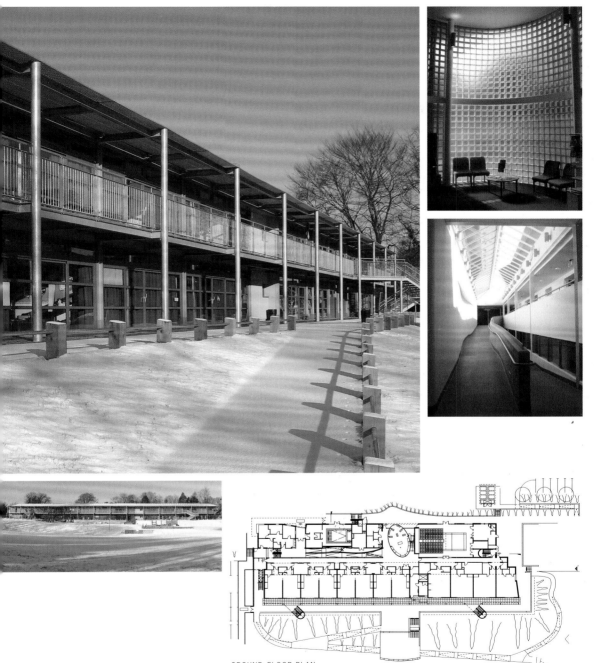

GROUND-FLOOR PLAN

PRIVATE ESTATE
.BERKSHIRE .DSDHA WITH LEROY STREET STUDIO (NEW YORK)

The family acquired this 161-hectare estate in 1998 and invited two firms that had first collaborated ten years ago (for the same client) to create a home from a disparate collection of more than 20 nineteenth-century brick buildings, ranging from stables to staff cottages.

Reoccupation of each of the structures within the stable courtyard with a single use reclaims both the individual buildings and the space of the courtyard as the unifying armature around which the recreational functions are woven: the dining hall, the children's house, and the pool and gymnasium. Any doubts there may have been about the pragmatic inconvenience of moving without protection between the buildings in adverse weather are instantly dispelled by the spatial clarity that the absence of such protection brings.

All the interiors are skilfully reoccupied and fit like gifts within gift-wrapping. Internally, the uses have a one-to-one relationship with the spaces in which they are housed. This imparts an instant legibility to each of the spaces: the temple, the dolls' house and the pool house – where, when the former stable doors are pinned back, the building appears to be flooded.

The minimalist spatial and material presence of the interiors and the quality of the workmanship simultaneously counterpoint and mirror the straightforward functionality of the existing structures. The unexpected is introduced through new full-height openings in the unseen elevations. These windows extend the interior through axial vistas, punctuated with sculpture, landscaping and 'vista framing' articulations to the horizon.

The spaces are minimally and elegantly detailed, and are equally dramatic in natural and artificial light. While the complex is not poetry, it is very competent prose.

CLIENT PRIVATE
STRUCTURAL ENGINEER MERVYN BROWN ASSOCIATES LTD
SERVICES ENGINEER BEAVER BUILDING SERVICES
CONTRACTOR LAYBROOK HOMES
CONTRACT VALUE CONFIDENTIAL
COMPLETION DATE JULY 2003
GROSS INTERNAL AREA POOL, 407 SQUARE METRES/HALL, 93 SQUARE METRES
PHOTOGRAPHER HÉLÈNE BINET

SLOANE ROBINSON BUILDING, KEBLE COLLEGE .OXFORD .RICK MATHER ARCHITECTS

Rick Mather has built at Keble before, so he is used to dealing with the eccentricities of the great Victorian architect William Butterfield. The new building – containing a multi-purpose theatre seating 250, dining and common room, music room, six seminar rooms and twenty study-bedrooms – completes the college quad, facing Mather's building of 1995 and incorporating an amphitheatre of lawn and a screen of mature trees. The use of non-load-bearing bricks is an appropriate contextual cross-reference to, and reinterpretation of, Butterfield's 'decorative façades'.

The essential orthogonal simplicity of the new building relates to the overall geometrical ordering of the college and provides a contrapuntal frame for the stair sculpture that can be seen spiralling vertically through the full height of the building. The stair is both the literal and metaphorical conveyor of movement. Its landings frame a dynamic sequence of views of the New Quad and the college, with St Michael at its apex.

Both internally and externally, the detailing is elegant, restrained, and consistent in quality with the existing college. Internally, the building is organized in a very straightforward manner, and is easy to use and understand. All the spaces reflect their current use and their capacity to be reinterpreted over time – whether they be restaurant, theatre, seminar room or study-bedroom.

The building incorporates innovative low-energy strategies, including a groundwater heating/cooling exchange system cast into the foundations, using the entire surface of the 20-metre-deep piles to collect and distribute ground heat – a system that is, of course, reversed in summer. The running costs are estimated to be a third those of a conventional air-based system.

CLIENT KEBLE COLLEGE
STRUCTURAL ENGINEER DEWHURST MACFARLANE & PARTNERS
SERVICES ENGINEER ATELIER TEN
QS STOCKINGS AND CLARKE
CONTRACTOR BENFIELD & LOXLEY
CONTRACT VALUE £5.3 MILLION
COMPLETION DATE SEPTEMBER 2002
PHOTOGRAPHER KEITH COLLIE

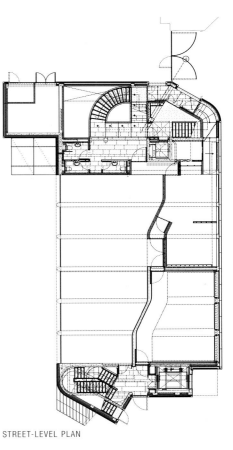

STREET-LEVEL PLAN

BUTTERFLY HOUSE
.DUNSFOLD .LAURIE CHETWOOD, CHETWOOD ASSOCIATES

In the Butterfly House bespoke contemporary art meets architecture. It is an extraordinary project, converted from a 1930s kit property, first built at the Ideal Home Show, dismantled and re-erected in a leafy Surrey lane in 1948.

The family noticed when living in the unchanged house in the 1990s that they were surrounded by butterflies. An ecological report confirmed that the 1.2-hectare site was a perfect habitat for the insects, and the family set about enhancing it with further planting. The report also produced the seed of a mad idea: the creation of a house inspired by the lifecycle of the butterfly.

This is a Bartlett project that somehow escaped and got built, an art installation as much as a house, wrapped around a largely unchanged building. The butterfly theme is followed throughout the house where the architect-owner and his designer wife have created a most unusual home including the furniture, made from glass, Perspex and suspended elasticated and rigid ties. The project involved 2 kilometres of bungee rope, 50 carbon-fibre fishing rods (for handrails) and 100 metres of fibre-optic cable that make the house, if anything, even more astonishing at night than by day. Everything is experimental, daring, prototypical and was carefully modelled and remodelled before construction.

Unsurprisingly, this was a scheme that divided the judges, but the architect deserves praise for the way that art and design have been integrated in this building. Innovation and experimentation are the key drivers behind the design vision and they have created a truly different building. It must be tremendous fun to grow up in this piece of inhabited architectural sculpture.

CLIENT PRIVATE
STRUCTURAL ENGINEERS WSP/GLEDSDALE ASSOCIATES/FURNESS GREEN PARTNERSHIP
SERVICES ENGINEER CHRISTOPHER BETTS ENVIRONMENTAL BIOLOGY
CONTRACTOR CRISP INTERIORS
CONTRACT VALUE £500,000
COMPLETION DATE SEPTEMBER 2003
GROSS INTERNAL AREA 225 SQUARE METRES
PHOTOGRAPHER EDMUND SUMNER – VIEW

SHORTLISTED FOR THE MANSER MEDAL

LA CONCHA, VILLE BAUDU
.VALE, GUERNSEY .MOOARC

To convert a derelict fifteenth-century barn into a contemporary home would be an achievement anywhere; to do so in this rigorously conservative planning environment is all the more remarkable. Through careful restoration and sympathetic but distinctly contemporary extension, the architect has provided himself and his family with a flexible home with office accommodation that allows fluidity of movement between old and new, inside and out.

Central to the plan is the large kitchen/living-room, with mezzanine sitting-room. All the ground-floor rooms have direct access into the garden, linking interior and exterior.

Detailing is clever and immaculate. Sliding screens open up and link rooms at will. The entire building is spacious and full of light and the glazed central ridge gives openness and vibrancy. This first-floor glass link between old barn and new extension and the opaque glass in the wall opposite neighbouring properties are examples of creative responses to planning constraints.

Energy conservation and the use of eco-friendly materials are keys to this project. Both the granite and the glass-resin floor are recycled. Throughout the house, thought has gone into creating ample storage space. The master bedroom on the first floor has a beautifully detailed bathroom separated from the sleeping area by a delightful curved wall of cupboards.

All this was achieved at a building cost of £1166 per square metre – a remarkable price on an island where most materials have to be imported.

CLIENT PRIVATE
STRUCTURAL ENGINEER THE DON BABBÉ PRACTICE
CONTRACTOR CBR DEVELOPMENTS LTD
CONTRACT VALUE £280,000
COMPLETION DATE NOVEMBER 2002
GROSS INTERNAL AREA 240 SQUARE METRES
PHOTOGRAPHER KARL TAYLOR

SHORTLISTED FOR THE STEPHEN LAWRENCE PRIZE

ROLLS-ROYCE MANUFACTURING PLANT AND HEAD OFFICE
.WESTHAMPNETT .GRIMSHAW

Rolls-Royce chose to site their new manufacturing plant and headquarters at Westhampnett, near Goodwood (far from industrial Crewe), because it has good transport links, not least with mainland Europe, and because of the testing facilities available at the nearby motor circuit. The facilities – all 55,000 square metres of them – are arranged around a central courtyard, accessed by a sweeping driveway reminiscent of the gravelled drives of the stately houses that many of the cars made here will grace.

The first impression is of quiet elegance, carefully set in a controlled landscape that will in time mature around the building and help to minimize its intrusion in the wider landscape. The attention to detail is stunning and the building is wonderfully inspirational, exuding confidence and pleasure. Everything, from the entrance pavilion for visitors with its finely crafted details using durable materials to the double-height production-line building, speaks of quality. Overlooking the production lines, a mezzanine floor accommodates training and workshop facilities, where apprentices learn the crafts of leather- and woodworking.

This is an egalitarian building (even if its products are not); it is clearly as pleasant for a production-line worker as for an executive. The staff facilities are made from quality materials and have an air of understated elegance. The detailing and quality of the production areas are not inferior to those found in the more public parts of the building. State-of-the-art technology is complemented in the interiors by the tasteful use of classic furniture.

The company has a good green transport policy, so car parking is limited. The building uses other environmentally aware methods, such as a sedum roof and water recycling, to reduce its impact on the surroundings. The factory has achieved an 'excellent' BREEAM rating.

CLIENT ROLLS-ROYCE MOTOR CARS LTD
STRUCTURAL ENGINEERS WSP/BMW GROUP/ CAMERON TAYLOR BEDFORD
SERVICES ENGINEER BURO HAPPOLD
QS DAVIS LANGDON
CONTRACTOR BMW GROUP
CONTRACT VALUE CONFIDENTIAL
COMPLETION DATE MAY 2003
GROSS INTERNAL AREA 55,000 SQUARE METRES
PHOTOGRAPHER EDMUND SUMNER – VIEW

ALSO ON STIRLING PRIZE MIDLIST

GROUND-FLOOR PLAN

85 SOUTHWARK STREET
.LONDON SE1 .ALLIES AND MORRISON

Building their own offices presents architects with an opportunity to demonstrate their skills free from the influence of patrons. This ambitious building shows Allies and Morrison's skills at many levels. On the macro scale the planning accommodates a new pedestrian route through the site that should reinforce much-needed public links from Tate Modern to further south.

The building itself follows a typical Corbusian section with a predominantly public base (which will be enhanced by a café), studio accommodation on the middle floors and a communal terrace protected by a screen wall on the roof. Unlike Le Corbusier's prototypical buildings, this one is well integrated as part of the streetscape.

The success of the predominantly glazed street elevation is partly due to the bright-yellow vertical shutters. These can be adjusted to vary privacy and light levels adjacent to individual workstations. Seen from outside, they create an enjoyable random rhythm and contrast well with the screen wall to the top floor, which has no windows facing the street. Overhanging louvres bounce light on to the north-facing surface, creating a sense of calm among the clutter of the surrounding roofscapes. The screen wall shelters the roof terrace and creates a delightful suntrap.

The extensive use of carefully honed exposed concrete creates a robust but refined interior. Other clients may have baulked at the cost of achieving this, but perhaps the result will encourage more developers to accept the benefits of exposed-concrete soffits – a simple way of using thermal mass to reduce cooling loads.

Each studio floor has a similar layout but is given variety by a stepping atrium on the south side with planted terraces above. This gives an internal volume to link the floors and encourages a sense of community. It also mean that a small area of external planting is visible from each workstation. The architects describe this device as a response to light-angle constraints, but, as in many well-designed buildings, a legal constraint has been turned to advantage.

CLIENT ALLIES AND MORRISON
STRUCTURAL ENGINEER WHITBYBIRD
SERVICES ENGINEER WSP GROUP
QS BARRY TANKEL PARTNERSHIP/
DAVIS LANGDON
CONTRACTOR MANSELL
FIT-OUT CONTRACTOR SPECTRUM PROJECTS
CONTRACT VALUE CONFIDENTIAL
COMPLETION DATE JUNE 2003
GROSS INTERNAL AREA 2284 SQUARE
METRES
PHOTOGRAPHER DENNIS GILBERT – VIEW

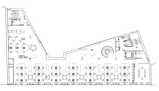

BRIDGE OF ASPIRATION
.LONDON WC2 .WILKINSON EYRE ARCHITECTS

The imaginative bridge linking the Royal Ballet School and the Royal Opera House evokes the spirit of the ballet dancers who use it. It has a wonderful quality of light and is thoughtfully detailed. Suspended in mid-air, extremely slender and totally elegant, this twisting bridge is both glazed and opaque, so as you walk across you get a half view, which then continues on the other side of the bridge. Already established as an icon of the area, in some ways the bridge is quite unobtrusive: people can walk underneath without seeing it.

Glass, timber and aluminium provide a structure that is elegant and transparent. It is a bold design for such an historical location but works extraordinarily well. It is well executed and exceptional. This is a structure that serves its function perfectly: not only is it a physical link between the Royal Ballet School and the Royal Opera House, but it is also slightly warm inside, so that the dancers (in their tutus and tights) don't get cold between the buildings.

This little project demonstrates that Wilkinson Eyre can operate at all scales and produce work that is entirely appropriate to context and to the needs of the client. It is every bit as perfect in its way as their Stirling Prize-winning Millennium Bridge in Gateshead. Called the Bridge of Aspiration, it is in fact total inspiration.

CLIENT THE ROYAL BALLET SCHOOL
STRUCTURAL ENGINEER FLINT & NEILL PARTNERSHIP
SERVICES ENGINEER BURO HAPPOLD
LIGHTING DESIGNER SPEIRS AND MAJOR ASSOCIATES
SPECIALIST BRIDGE CONTRACTOR GIG FASSADENBAU
CONTRACTOR BENSON LTD
CONTRACT VALUE £800,000
COMPLETION DATE FEBRUARY 2003
GROSS INTERNAL AREA 35 SQUARE METRES
PHOTOGRAPHER NICK WOOD

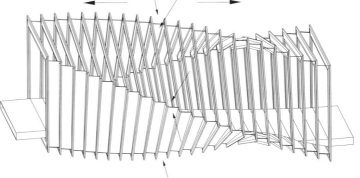

DIAGRAM SHOWING GLAZING
INSTALLATION

CITY INN WESTMINSTER
.LONDON SW1 .BENNETTS ASSOCIATES

This elegantly detailed hotel is a clever piece of urban infill that makes a significant contribution to the public realm. A refreshing contrast to the proliferation of new structures close to the River Thames shouting for attention, this building is handsome and confident without being too showy, and it really does something for the city, creating a delightful new route to the river.

The deep-blue terracotta cladding and generous overhanging louvred canopy are enough to distinguish the hotel from its nondescript neighbours. The classical composition of the elevations is gentle and subtle. Unlike many contemporary street façades, this one deserves more than a quick glance. From the street, the hotel appears to fill the entire site, restoring the definition of John Islip Street and Thorney Street that has been lacking over the long period when it was vacant. However, the plan is more complex than is apparent at first sight. It comprises three interconnected blocks where the irregular site geometry is neatly accommodated by the glazed circulation core. This configuration offers excellent views to the outside from each lift landing, making orientation easier than in many hotels of comparable scale.

This project is clearly a team effort. Artwork – the best by Susanna Heron – has been sensitively incorporated in the new pedestrian space. The interior design, although carried out by another consultant, is seamlessly integrated with the architecture. The use of colour is consistently bold: the deep-blue exterior is complemented by the extensive use of red inside, sometimes in surprising places such as a WC cubicle or on a bedroom ceiling. The roof-level plant has been neatly screened and the lift over-run is concealed from view by a rooftop meeting room that exploits, for the time being at least, spectacular views across the West End.

CLIENT CITY INN
ART CONSULTANT MODUS OPERANDI
ARTIST SUSANNA HERON
INTERIOR DESIGN PROOF CONSULTING
STRUCTURAL ENGINEER BLYTH & BLYTH CONSULTING ENGINEERS
SERVICES ENGINEER FABER MAUNSELL
QS FAITHFUL & GOULD
CONTRACTOR CARILLION BUILDING
CONTRACT VALUE £35 MILLION
COMPLETION DATE AUGUST 2003
GROSS INTERNAL AREA 20,983 SQUARE METRES
PHOTOGRAPHER PETER COOK – VIEW

THE DAVIDSON BUILDING
.LONDON WC2 .LIFSCHUTZ DAVIDSON

The Davidson Building, named after Ian Davidson, the architect who died tragically young in 2003, is an eight-storey new-build structure behind a retained Edwardian façade that has been reinforced with stainless-steel post-tensioned ties. Westminster planners insisted on its retention and added an unusual condition: that the Exeter Street façade should use white-glazed brick to bounce light back into the Strand Palace Hotel. The result is nice, tidy, flexible office space, designed to be let either as a whole building or just floor by floor.

Office buildings behind retained façades normally present difficult architectural problems as the levels of the new floors don't match the original windows, not least because of the need to accommodate modern services. This building solves the problem in a unique and effortless way. It creates a gap behind the façade and sets the floors back from the perimeter behind a 3-metre-wide atrium. The clean floorplates it provides are bright and light. The exposed soffits allow for a generous 2.85 metres of headroom. The attractive white Carrara marble entrance with leather panelling on walls and in the lifts, and the sliding doors to the entrance, all give off air of affluent calm.

It is a wonderful use of an existing building. The new wall to the rear is elegantly detailed with opening windows to allow natural ventilation – unusual for such a location. It is also highly energy efficient in its use of tempered rather than chilled air. The use of exposed-concrete soffits with their high thermal capacity reduces temperature swings – just one of the tricks Alex Lifschutz and Ian Davidson learnt when working on Foster's Hongkong & Shanghai Bank.

CLIENT DERWENT VALLEY
STRUCTURAL ENGINEER ARUP
SERVICES ENGINEER ARUP
QS DAVIS LANGDON
CONTRACTOR YJL CONSTRUCTION
CONTRACT VALUE £15.5 MILLION
COMPLETION DATE FEBRUARY 2003
GROSS INTERNAL AREA 4645 SQUARE METRES
PHOTOGRAPHER RICHARD BRYANT – ARCAID

SHORTLISTED FOR THE RIBA SUSTAINABILITY AWARD

DOUBLE HOUSE
.LONDON NW3 .WOOLF ARCHITECTS

Double House – two houses of similar design for two brothers – is the product of an RIBA competition. The two families can share space and yet have privacy when it is required. This is communal living in a whole new sense. The brothers both work from home in an office at the front of the house, which also houses the ceramics studio of one of their wives.

The scheme – a labour of love by the architects – has exceptional quality. It makes good use of the landscaped 9-metre-deep sloping site and it has an almost spiritual quality. The pool under the house is a truly remarkable space. The pool, the plant room and the gym, also in the basement, are the only shared areas in the house.

Originally the clients wanted simple white boxes, but the architect persuaded them to accept a greyish-brown handmade brick. This will age beautifully and picks up on the bark of the trees that are so important to the context. The house, with its large areas of glass and rooflights that open up directly to the sky, has a great feeling of being in the garden, breaking down the barriers of inside and outside. The accommodation is simply organized around two sliding-roofed atria, with the rooms facing outwards. The lightwell extends down to bring light into the pool. The quality of natural light throughout is serene.

Although called Double House, this is really two externally identical houses – Upper House and Lower House – and each has one of the dominant mature trees (beech and oak) that had to be retained in the garden. Internally it is a different matter, as each family has stamped its personality on the layout, décor and furnishings. These are perhaps the most luxurious back-to-back houses ever built.

CLIENT PRIVATE
STRUCTURAL ENGINEER PRICE & MYERS
SERVICES ENGINEER FURNESS GREEN PARTNERSHIP
QS CAPITA SYMONDS
CONTRACTOR BLUESTONE PLC
CONTRACT VALUE £2.8 MILLION
COMPLETION DATE JULY 2003
GROSS INTERNAL AREA 1000 SQUARE METRES
PHOTOGRAPHER MATTHEW WEINREB

ALSO ON STIRLING PRIZE MIDLIST AND SHORTLISTED FOR THE ARCHITECTS' JOURNAL FIRST BUILDING AWARD

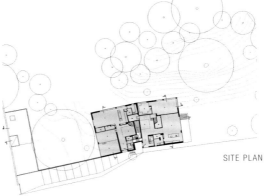

SITE PLAN

EMPRESS STATE BUILDING
.LONDON SW6 .WILKINSON EYRE ARCHITECTS

The 100-metre-high Empress State is the tallest building in Hammersmith and Fulham and one of the 30 tallest in London. It is not easy converting one of the capital's more brutish towers, with a number of quirks working against it, but the architects have demonstrated how a difficult building can be transformed into highly lettable space (it is now home to the Metropolitan Police's PR department). In effect, the Empress State has become a new product.

Built on the site of an enormous ferris wheel erected in 1896 and adjoining the Earl's Court exhibition halls, the Empress State's original architects were Stone, Toms and Partners. Built in 1961 for the Admiralty, it remained a Ministry of Defence property until 1998, when the Arms Procurement Department finally left.

The distinctive Y-shaped plan with curved façades has been retained. On the main south elevation a 5.5-metre extension has been added between floors 3 and 26 to produce bigger floorplates. The entire south façade has also been reclad, incorporating elegant external shading. The anodized aerofoil louvres form a continuous screen that both unifies and articulates the façade while also providing much-needed protection from the sun. On the existing east and west elevations low-'E' solar-controlled double-glazed 1.65-metre-wide units replace 1.1-metre-wide single-glazed windows.

Plant has been relocated at a lower level, making imaginative new rooftop accommodation possible. The architects have created a new series of spaces and incorporated a revolving restaurant to take advantage of the views. Additionally, a lot of clever refurbishment has been done at different levels throughout the building to increase the area of office space. The whole site has been relandscaped, with a traffic-free piazza intended as a new public space. Planting helps to soften this area.

CLIENT LAND SECURITIES
STRUCTURAL ENGINEER ANTHONY HUNT ASSOCIATES
MECHANICAL ENGINEER MG PARTNERSHIP
ELECTRICAL ENGINEER BWS PARTNERSHIP
QS E C HARRIS
CONTRACTOR BOVIS LEND LEASE
CONTRACT VALUE £84 MILLION
COMPLETION DATE JULY 2003
GROSS INTERNAL AREA 38,563 SQUARE METRES
PHOTOGRAPHER EDMUND SUMNER – VIEW

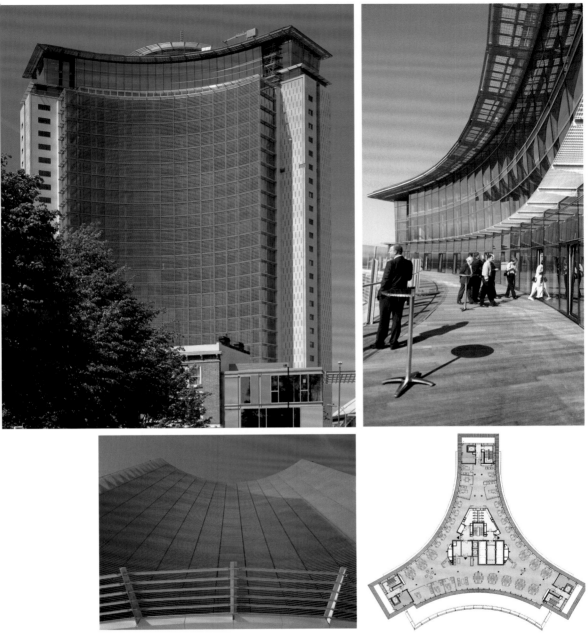

28TH-FLOOR PLAN

GAINSBOROUGH STUDIOS
.LONDON N1 .MUNKENBECK + MARSHALL

This is a development of three blocks of middle- to upper-income housing: two new blocks and one (the affordable housing) that is the reconstituted former Gainsborough film studios. The development forms a square, with one block lining the Grand Union Canal.

The square is dominated by a giant corten-steel Alfred Hitchcock head (by Anthony Donaldson) on a plinth of the same material. This reveals itself to be a small office suite on one side. The ground level is developed as a series of lettable elements that can be offices, studios or rehearsal spaces. The ground areas of square and canal boardwalk are linked by well-designed stairways incorporating waterfalls and various urban devices.

The overall impression is of a development of an unusually high level of design, sustained from penthouse suite through to affordable apartment. Each is consistently well thought through with neat, unfussy detailing, good use of space, fine views, and a generally sophisticated but not insistent atmosphere. This has been carried through to such elements as the entrances, demonstrating that the architects have clearly understood the issues of first impression, clarity and space supervision.

Within the parameters of a commercial venture, this project should be seen as a marker for elegant design and town-making.

CLIENT LINCOLN HOLDINGS
STRUCTURAL ENGINEER ELLIS + MOORE
SERVICES ENGINEER MAX FORDHAM LLP
QS DEARLING ASSOCIATES
CONTRACTOR YJL CONSTRUCTION
CONTRACT VALUE £35.5 MILLION
COMPLETION DATE DECEMBER 2003
GROSS INTERNAL AREA 27,400 SQUARE METRES
PHOTOGRAPHER MORLEY VON STERNBERG

GROUND-FLOOR PLAN

GORMLEY STUDIO .LONDON N7 .DAVID CHIPPERFIELD ARCHITECTS

Hidden among the barren railway lands to the north of King's Cross is a calm, secret, white building forming the backdrop to a calm, controlled yard for a clever and prolific artist, the sculptor Antony Gormley. The white face of the building is effectively a fretted profile that recalls that of the saw-toothed north-lit roof of an industrial shed. In fact this profile does not face north–south at all and must therefore be considered iconic. In many ways, this place has the feel of a gallery, but then the conditions best suited for the making of art are less different from those required for its display than is often thought.

Two giant galvanized-steel staircases rise from the centre and link to the more private studios and offices used by the artist and his artist wife. These are also highly iconic and permit no compromise by way of supporting legs or other impedimenta. They are striking pieces of sculpture in their own right. There are no internal staircases, making the sculptor and his assistants actors in a drama whose comings and goings lead to the dénouement of another beautiful piece of art.

Below and within are the main production spaces, which are clear, well-lit and obviously the result of a careful brief. Client and architect, who already knew each other well, worked closely together, and the resulting installation is very specific, and thus appropriate.

The studios – both those for general production and those of a more private nature – have exactly the atmosphere of basic calm combined with toughness that is preferred for work (and escape) by many artists.

Detailing has the level of discrimination and elegance expected of this firm, and is entirely appropriate. The result is deliberate, uncompromising and total, re-establishing that special atmosphere for art that we remember from the now-abandoned Saatchi Gallery in St John's Wood.

CLIENT ANTONY GORMLEY
STRUCTURAL ENGINEER JANE WERNICK ASSOCIATES
SERVICES ENGINEER ENVIRONMENTAL ENGINEERING PARTNERSHIP
QS CAPITA
CONTRACTOR LEONARD FIELD GROUP
CONTRACT VALUE CONFIDENTIAL
COMPLETION DATE AUGUST 2003
GROSS INTERNAL AREA 909 SQUARE METRES
PHOTOGRAPHER RICHARD BRYANT – ARCAID

ALSO ON STIRLING PRIZE MIDLIST

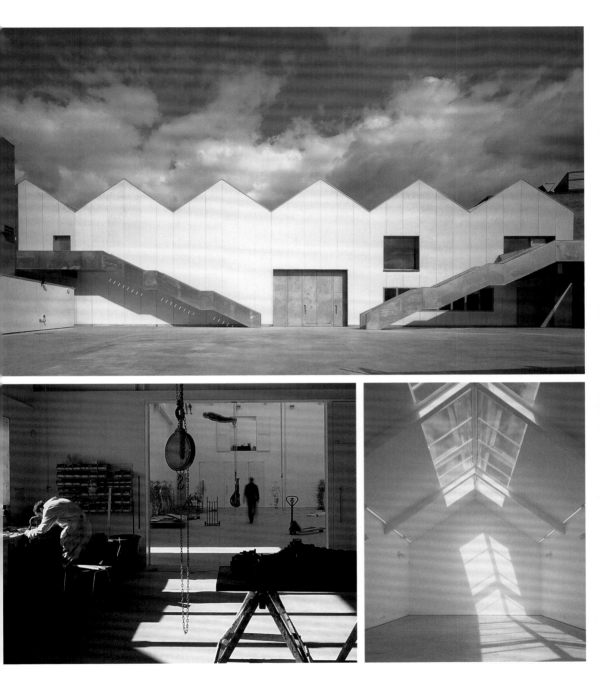

GRADUATE CENTRE, LONDON METROPOLITAN UNIVERSITY
.LONDON N7 .STUDIO DANIEL LIBESKIND

It is impossible to treat this building dispassionately, as if it were just some odd piece of academic development. It is unashamedly a 'landmark' gesture by an aspiring but hitherto modest institution.

Ironically, this high-art object finds itself in one of the grottier high streets of inner London – the Holloway Road. It was intended to give a clear focus to the university, not merely in PR terms but also physically, as a centre for graduate students previously scattered around the campus. Even more practically, the brief called for a discrete building that could be accessed from the street by those attending conferences or other extramural activities. Materially and substantially the building responds to all this well. The Libeskind language of form announces itself to the street and presents a clear entrance, some sharp folds and cuts. There is a useful outcrop in the form of a well-guarded balcony, from which (presumably) heroic philosophical or political statements could be declaimed.

This is a concrete-framed structure; that and a stainless-steel cladding with relatively few openings have produced a low-energy building. Inside, the concrete is exposed; other finishes are equally simple and robust.

The building fulfils its external obligations perfectly well but inevitably a level of expectation has been established by the Jewish Museum in Berlin. In fact the window cuts here or a staircase there give only glimpses of the same magic.

The building's importance is as an *initiative* as much as a finished article – it is to be hoped that it will challenge the relative conservatism of most London institutions. The clients are to be highly congratulated.

CLIENT LONDON METROPOLITAN UNIVERSITY
STRUCTURAL ENGINEER CADOGAN TIETZ
SERVICES ENGINEER WSP GROUP
QS GLEEDS
CONTRACTOR COSTAIN
CONTRACT VALUE £3 MILLION
COMPLETION DATE FEBRUARY 2004
GROSS INTERNAL AREA 760 SQUARE METRES
PHOTOGRAPHER BITTER BREDT FOTOGRAFIE

GROUND-FLOOR PLAN

THE HORNIMAN MUSEUM AND GARDENS .LONDON SE23 .ALLIES AND MORRISON

In 1998 Allies and Morrison were appointed to reinstate the integrity and legibility of the Horniman Museum and to improve facilities for visitors. This project responds well to the challenge of extending the existing building by Charles Townsend (architect also of the Whitechapel Art Gallery).

The original museum had become surrounded by ad-hoc extensions and disconnected from some delightful adjacent gardens. Rather than adopt a low-key or subservient approach, the new part of the museum provides a companion to the original that is of equal stature. The space between new and old has been cleared to provide both a focus for the museum in the form of a covered courtyard and a means of integrating retained structures – a conservatory terminating an axial vista from the courtyard on one side, and a gallery on the other.

Externally, the extension follows the form of the existing museum, but reinterprets the detailing in an appropriately contemporary manner. This is most successful on the side elevations where the zinc roof detailing is particularly well done. The brickwork is also well proportioned and the entrance is clearly articulated.

Inside, the complex level changes have been neatly resolved. Stone floors in the public areas reinforce the links between original building, extension and outdoor spaces. Natural and artificial light are well handled, giving a smooth transition between the brighter circulation spaces and the darker galleries where the illumination of exhibits takes precedence.

The tied-arched structure is elegantly expressed, and it is good to see that the horizontal ties are not sagging. It would have been unfortunate if the structure of a building housing so many fine musical instruments had not itself been finely tuned.

CLIENT HORNIMAN MUSEUM
STRUCTURAL ENGINEER WHITBYBIRD
SERVICES ENGINEER MAX FORDHAM & PARTNERS
QS DAVIS LANGDON
CONTRACTOR COSTAIN LTD
CONTRACT VALUE £8 MILLION
COMPLETION DATE JULY 2002
GROSS INTERNAL AREA 2250 SQUARE METRES
PHOTOGRAPHER PETER COOK – VIEW

SHORTLISTED FOR THE RIBA INCLUSIVE DESIGN AWARD

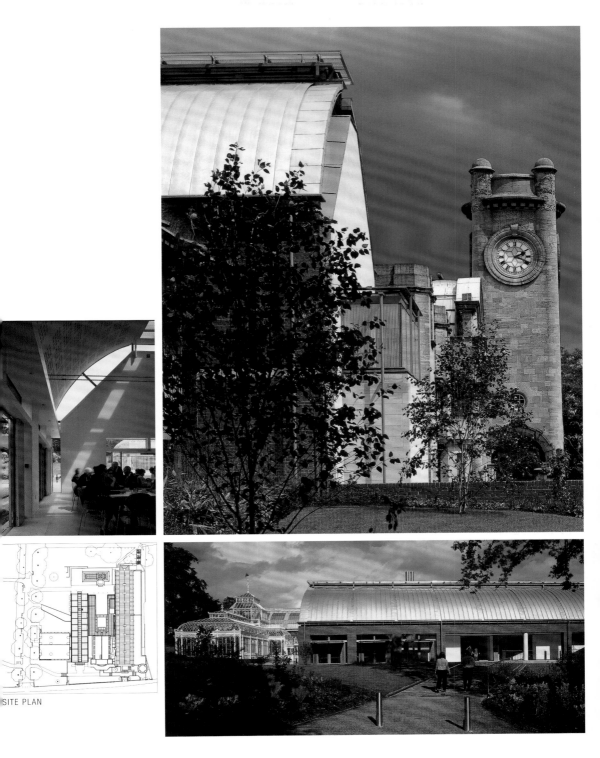

SITE PLAN

MILLBANK MILLENNIUM PIER
.LONDON SW1 .MARKS BARFIELD ARCHITECTS

It seems appropriate that the starting point for a river link between two art galleries – Tates Britain and Modern – should simultaneously take the form of a moored vessel, a sculpture and a pier. Also fittingly, the new riverboat service stops off at another fine piece of architecture-cum-engineering, the same practice's London Eye.

Structurally, the landing-stage and linking gangway are superbly integrated. The gangway forms part of the anchoring system in conjunction with an innovative system of radial struts. The traditional anchoring device of vertical dolphins seen on most landing stages seems clumsy by comparison.

The pier's grey steel organic form, constructed from simple flat plates, evokes comparison with HMS *Belfast* moored further downstream, and recognizes that the various structures and craft moored on the River Thames are as much part of the cityscape as the adjacent buildings.

The functions of bridge, landing-stage, steps and shelter have been beautifully combined into a simple sculptural form that is both intimate in scale and dynamic in appearance. Like any good sculpture, the visual qualities change from different viewpoints, and this dynamic is enhanced by an active lighting scheme, called *Tidal*, that shifts between chartreuse and blue with the ebb and flow of the tide, giving the pier an ethereal, almost alien quality at night; by day it is rather more business-like. The other light installation is entitled *Flash*, an evocation of the scatter-gun effect of the flashguns of the paparazzi. Angela Bulloch worked closely with the architects and the construction team from the outset to produce a lighting scheme that is integral to the project as a whole.

The creativity of this scheme extends to the finer details, such as a maintenance ladder formed by neat trapezoidal cut-outs in the steel-plate hull, a practical solution that enriches the visual grain. This project works brilliantly in both concept and in detail.

CLIENT LONDON RIVER SERVICES
ARTIST ANGELA BULLOCH
MARINE STRUCTURAL ENGINEER BECKETT RANKINE PARTNERSHIP
SERVICES ENGINEER PHILLIPSONS
SPECIALIST LIGHTING DESIGNED ARCHITECTURAL LIGHTING
SPECIALIST STEELWORK CONTRACTOR K & N WELDING
CONTRACTOR MOWLEM MARINE
CONTRACT VALUE £1.82 MILLION
COMPLETION DATE MAY 2003
GROSS INTERNAL AREA 110 SQUARE METRES
PHOTOGRAPHER NICK WOOD

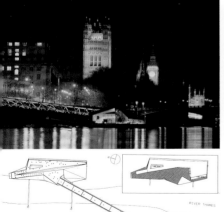

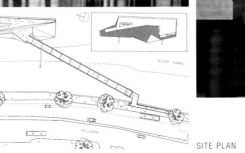

SITE PLAN

PLATFORM 1 KING'S CROSS COMMUNITY LEARNING CENTRE
. LONDON N1 .GOLLIFER LANGSTON ARCHITECTS

This is a community learning centre in a tough corner of London. It is all about language and communication, unsurprisingly perhaps, since 40 languages are spoken in the immediate vicinity. It provides a library, a learning centre, language-teaching rooms, a multimedia recording studio, facilities for the study of the development of language, a crèche and even a film studio.

A basic rectangular space, efficiently and straightforwardly interpreted, it is perhaps most reminiscent of the committed nonchalance of the best of British school buildings of the 1950s – but tougher. An essay in making a cheap-and-cheerful building, it sets three simple curved corner elements within the rectangle: one a big rooflight over the entrance, one a control space, and one (outside) the infants' playroom. These are colourful and chirpy devices, and the infants' pavilion, in particular, is preferable to other more ponderous examples of the genre. The classrooms, the film studio, the entrance/reading room, and the other spaces, all work extremely well.

One amusing element remains from the world of formal architecture – the tiny slab of glass that sits above the entrance as a marker. Glass is employed elsewhere more practically. Because the building is used by girls from a local school and at the same time by adults, there was a need to make a physical distinction between different areas, while still allowing the spaces to flow from one to another. The solution is a play between the glazed and solid elements.

The building uses passive cooling and natural ventilation, with a wind tower over the main double-height space to draw air from the learning space below.

CLIENT ELIZABETH GARRET ANDERSON SCHOOL
STRUCTURAL ENGINEER BURO HAPPOLD
SERVICES ENGINEER BURO HAPPOLD
QS MELLISH & LYNCH
CONTRACTOR DURKAN PUDELEK
CONTRACT VALUE £1.35 MILLION
COMPLETION DATE AUGUST 2003
GROSS INTERNAL AREA 1030 SQUARE METRES
PHOTOGRAPHER JAMES BRITTAIN (LEFT)/ TIM SOAR (RIGHT)

GROUND-FLOOR PLAN

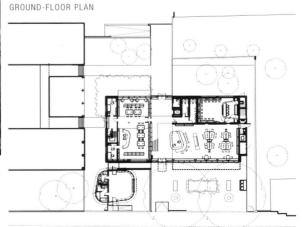

RAINES COURT
.LONDON N16 .ALLFORD HALL MONAGHAN MORRIS

This Peabody Trust mixed-ownership development of housing with some live-and-work elements at ground level uses a high proportion of unit prefabrication in the construction and articulates this by way of its tough, exposed-steel structure. This is high-density urban living with 594 habitable rooms per hectare (against a UDP guideline of 250). It is the largest prefabricated scheme built to date and the first Housing Corporation-funded modular scheme anywhere in the country. But, in the spirit of Egan, The Peabody Trust is interested in the efficiencies resulting from careful supply-chain management. So it's an experiment, but one that's still good to live in and good to look at.

The view from the street is of a powerful, even uncompromising, block. The revelation from the courtyard side and particularly from higher levels is of a very well-considered and agreeable ambience for urban living. The balconies that thrust out into the court show genuine and delightful evidence of family life – they are effectively large outside yards.

The apartments themselves are fine too – not elaborate but well considered. They work well and give good views within and without. The dedicated outside space (between apartment and access balcony), for bicycles, boxes and so on, is also a really good idea. The eight live-work units have the potential to be used as models for the ever-increasing home-working market.

The building is really quite tough: the steelwork is a joy to Constructivist taste and definitely 'in yer face'. A true piece of urban housing for an uncompromising world that is, deep within, very real and very humane.

CLIENT THE PEABODY TRUST
MODULE MANUFACTURER YORKON LTD
STRUCTURAL ENGINEER WHITBYBIRD
SERVICES ENGINEER ENGINEERING DESIGN PARTNERSHIP
QS WALKER MANAGEMENT
LANDSCAPE ARCHITECT WATKINS DALLY
CONTRACTOR WATES CONSTRUCTION
CONTRACT VALUE £8.9 MILLION
COMPLETION DATE SEPTEMBER 2003
GROSS INTERNAL AREA 5871 SQUARE METRES
PHOTOGRAPHER TIM SOAR

THE PEABODY TRUST IS RIBA/ARTS COUNCIL ENGLAND CLIENT OF THE YEAR

GROUND-FLOOR PLAN

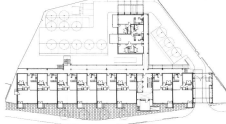

TRAFALGAR SQUARE AND ITS ENVIRONS, WORLD SQUARES FOR ALL
.LONDON W1 .FOSTER AND PARTNERS

The overall objective of unifying the National Gallery with Trafalgar Square along its northern edge has been successfully achieved, and, with its completion, the square has been transformed into a truly public and accessible urban space.

The hand of the architect is at first not very evident. The major moves are so consistent with the existing environment that to a casual visitor the new elements might seem always to have existed. But on closer examination the wealth of care and detail becomes apparent. This sense of continuity combined with contemporary details of material substance is commendable in such an historic environment.

The broad stair gently connects the pedestrianized street to the lower square and is singular and simple in its ambition and execution, cut from the same granite as the plinth. At street level the two pavilions of the disabled lifts sit discreetly, detailed with considerable care in solid bronze. Between street level and the square two new blocks have been inserted: a small café to the east and public WCs to the west – clearly the work of the architect. Huge bronze handrails on the new granite steps are helpful for partially disabled people.

It is clear that a long and careful consultation process has contributed to the success of the project. It demonstrates a strong contribution from all parties: the architect, Westminster planners, English Heritage and the GLA.

Trafalgar Square is vast, easily accommodating 8000 people, and is used for outside concerts, demonstrations, political gatherings, as a meeting point, for art installations and cultural events (not to mention its role as breeding-ground for pigeons). So everything has to be robust (which it is), accessible to all (which it is), and flexible (which it also is). The alterations have had a considerable effect on the life of the square and given back to London a public space of great quality and one worthy of its great setting.

CLIENTS GLA/TRANSPORT FOR LONDON
CONSERVATION ARCHITECT FEILDEN & MAWSON
LANDSCAPE AND URBAN DESIGN ATKINS DESIGN ENVIRONMENT & ENGINEERING
TRANSPORT PLANNING AND HIGHWAYS ENGINEERING ATKINS DESIGN ENVIRONMENT & ENGINEERING
LIGHTING CONSULTANT SPEIRS AND MAJOR ASSOCIATES
QS DAVIS LANGDON
ACCESS CONSULTANT JMU ACCESS PARTNERSHIP
CONTRACTOR FITZPATRICK
CONTRACT VALUE £25 MILLION
COMPLETION DATE JULY 2003
GROSS AREA 48,000 SQUARE METRES
PHOTOGRAPHER NIGEL YOUNG

SITE PLAN

BURDA CAR PARK
.OFFENBURG, GERMANY .INGENHOVEN UND PARTNER

To produce a building as substantial as a multi-storey car park and to make it as insubstantial as gossamer, as Ingenhoven und Partner have done here in Offenburg, is a remarkable achievement.

Round buildings are relatively less common than they were in Saxon times, despite computer-aided design. (There are three in this year's awards if you count the Dublin Spire). Car parks, though, do seem to be the ideal type for the configuration, if only because there is no furniture to make fit. The two independent helical ramps (one up, one down) for this five-storey 60-metre-diameter car park are cantilevered from a radial exposed-concrete core. The prefabricated-concrete parking decks are supported on prefabricated steel beams and propped at the rim by steel columns.

Thrown over this structure, like a duvet over a bed, is a translucent lattice of Oregon pine, which, on the roof deck, sheds a delightful play of light and shade across the floor, like a well-crafted pergola. The supporting cables are fixed by clips that swing to allow the screen to move in the way the branches of a tree sway and creak in a wind. As well as being beautiful, the solution is entirely practical: the traffic fumes that permeate most car parks are gently wafted away.

The result is a delight, a positive contribution to the ever-expanding campus of good buildings commissioned by media giant Burda, and, almost uniquely, a car park that is open, welcoming, even beautiful.

CLIENT HUBERT BURDA MEDIA HOLDING
STRUCTURAL ENGINEER WERNER SOBECK INGENIEURE
SERVICES ENGINEER HL-TECHNIK AG
CONTRACTOR WOLFF & MÜLLER
CONTRACT VALUE €4.7 MILLION
COMPLETION DATE JULY 2002
GROSS INTERNAL AREA 15,400 SQUARE METRES
PHOTOGRAPHER H G ESCH

GROUND-FLOOR PLAN

169 .EUROPEAN UNION

NORDDEUTSCHE LANDESBANK
.HANNOVER, GERMANY .BEHNISCH, BEHNISCH & PARTNER

The Norddeutsche Landesbank head office occupies a whole city block right at the heart of Hannover, providing accommodation for 1500 staff. The enormous scale of the brief and the size of the site could easily have resulted in an intimidating building, but the result is a delight, offering to those fortunate enough to work here an environment of exceptional quality, and to the city a welcoming, accessible and impressive landmark.

The ground floor is democratically given over to the public realm, with shops, café, art gallery and a landscaped courtyard threaded by footpaths through the site (open 24 hours a day), and a generous pool. All these elements exhibit an exuberant diagonal geometry that subverts the order of the urban block. At the heart of the site, a riot of canted glazed planes marks the entrance to the offices, with generous foyers and a staff cafeteria overlooking the courtyard, and a fine stone-paved stair that leads to further foyers at first-floor level. From here all wings of the offices can be reached by tubular glazed bridges. Above rises an extraordinary 18-storey tower of rotated and cantilevered floorplates, no two the same, culminating in exquisitely furnished dining-rooms and a conference- and boardroom enjoying spectacular views over the city. This is a building that accommodates the clients' corporate requirements, rather than fighting them.

The building is innovative in many respects: the jointless reinforced-concrete construction, the ecologically sensitive servicing (all offices are largely naturally lit and ventilated), the beautifully planted green roofscape, and the fully glazed elevations. Yet the building is shaped by man rather than by technology, and specially commissioned artworks are integrated throughout the site.

Playful, even wilful in places, the building offers a fine and highly individual presence to the city, an inventive new standard of office environment that avoids the monotony of current corporate plush, and suggests more rewarding ways of working in the inner city.

CLIENT NORDDEUTSCHE LANDESBANK
STRUCTURAL ENGINEERS ARGE TRAGWERKSPLANUNG/WETZEL + VON SEHT WITH PFEFFERKORN + PARTNER
SERVICES ENGINEER ARGE TGA
ENERGY CONCEPT TRANSSOLAR ENERGIETECHNIK GMBH
CONTRACT VALUE € 193 MILLION
COMPLETION DATE 2002
GROSS INTERNAL AREA 75,000 SQUARE METRES
PHOTOGRAPHER ROLAND HASBE

ALSO ON STIRLING PRIZE MIDLIST

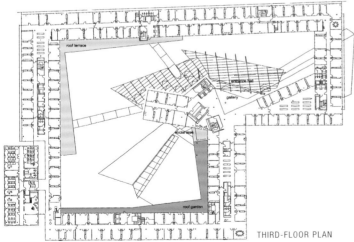

THIRD-FLOOR PLAN

171 .EUROPEAN UNION

HENNIGSDORF TOWN HALL
.HENNIGSDORF, GERMANY .SAUERBRUCH HUTTON ARCHITECTS

There is a growing tradition in Europe – including Ireland but with the sad and inevitable exception of the UK – of local authorities commissioning good council offices and chambers, where quality of design speaks of excellence of service. Here, Hennigsdorf, on the north-west edge of Berlin, in a depressed part of the former Soviet bloc, asked sauerbruch hutton to give them a building that would restore some local pride and form a bridge between the old and newer part of the town. They might have expected one of the practice's colourful signature buildings. If so, they must have been disappointed. But in removing the signature, they have proved what we knew all along, that here is a practice that can do it without the gestures. This understated building is one of their best.

It takes the form of a series of interconnecting ellipses. The main block rises three glass storeys behind a plinth faced with beautifully crafted hand-finished red brick, the glass element appearing to float effortlessly – a quality particularly noticeable when looking into the foyer from the council chamber. This contains all the main functions of the town hall arranged around and above a generous foyer, or 'Forum', which is used as a waiting and consultation area, with good architect-designed furniture providing privacy and a degree of luxury the majority of the building's users are surely unaccustomed to. The offices upstairs are double-skinned, allowing for a complex system of natural ventilation similar to that used in the practice's Biological Research Laboratories in Biberach (but without the colour). Between the inner and outer skins is a 30-cm gap with venetian blinds. These are controlled by the building-management system, which can be manually over-ridden.

The council chamber, the second ovoid, is an understated room with curved and delicately painted ceiling. (This pattern of soft blue and salmon pink is carried throughout the building.) Small parliaments would be content to sit here.

CLIENT CITY OF HENNIGSDORF
STRUCTURAL ENGINEER INGENIEURBÜRO FÜR BAUWESEN HERBERT FINK
SERVICES ENGINEER ZIBELL WILLNER & PARTNER
CONTRACTOR MÄRKISCHE INGENIEUR GMBH
CONTRACT VALUE £6.3 MILLION
COMPLETION DATE DECEMBER 2003
GROSS INTERNAL AREA 6211 SQUARE METRES
PHOTOGRAPHER BITTER BREDT FOTOGRAFIE

GROUND-FLOOR PLAN

173 .EUROPEAN UNION

GEK HEADQUARTERS
.ATHENS, GREECE .HOPKINS ARCHITECTS

Modern Athens is a uniformly dust-coloured concrete city. At first glance this new headquarters building for a Greek construction company – concrete-framed with glass and stainless-steel infills – blends into that setting, yet on closer inspection it is distinguished from it by its quality. Based on a powerful invited-competition-winning concept of 2000, it was designed and built in only 20 months, enforcing a discipline on client and architect that is palpable in every detail. For all that, it is a humane building.

The building sits among the extreme heat and noise of central Athens; its low-key entrance is off a hostile four-lane urban motorway between the city centre and the airport. The accommodation is arranged around an central open courtyard where environmental conditions are easier to control than in the busy surrounding streets. Once inside this lofty, cool, fan-shaped atrium, you are in an oasis of quiet and calm – and there is a distinctly non-corporate feel. This is achieved through the simplicity of materials (timber, concrete, and glass) and the fact that it is not only open-topped but also open to one side, with screened views on to neighbours' balconies, umbrellas and even washing lines. Far from turning its back on the city, it positively invites it in. All circulation is concentrated around the atrium, resulting in a lively scene of constant activity.

To cope with the effects of strong sunlight, glazing on the east- and west-facing elevations has been kept to a minimum, the remaining areas being encased in stainless-steel shading panels. The only sunlight allowed into working areas is reflected and shaded.

This building demonstrates the value of a truly committed client working with a dedicated architect to produce a thoughtful and sophisticated building.

CLIENT GEK-TERNA
STRUCTURAL ENGINEER P MADAS AND ASSOCIATES
SERVICES ENGINEER HLMME
CONTRACTOR TERNA
CONTRACT VALUE £4 MILLION
COMPLETION DATE 2002
GROSS INTERNAL AREA 11,000 SQUARE METRES
PHOTOGRAPHER HOPKINS ARCHITECTS

GROUND-FLOOR PLAN

175 .EUROPEAN UNION

HOWTH HOUSE
.CO DUBLIN, IRELAND .O'DONNELL + TUOMEY

This house sets out to make the most of its outstanding setting by focusing on specific views of the landscape – a goal it achieves in a relaxed and elegant way. Through the curving cross-walls of the plan the viewer is subtly directed towards the harbour and Ireland's Eye beyond, while the spaces between the walls connect effortlessly to one another and to the world outside.

Howth is a delightful family house, with an excellent appearance and views, and it makes a distinctive architectural contribution to its neighbourhood without trying to dominate. Clearly the result of a happy collaboration between committed client and sensitive architect, the house and its site have made the most of magnificent sea views, both from the main living spaces on the first floor and from bedrooms and balconies. While the site is no bigger than that of neighbouring properties, the provision of significant volumes of space in the main areas has given the house a very spacious feel, while the more intimate rooms still have access to views and external spaces. The wide variety of rooms and spaces has given the client the possibility of using the house in different ways at different times over a long period – the house is adaptable without requiring further work.

This is a house that will mature with its occupants. Materials are robust without being crude. Internally, well judged hardwood insertions set within the rough-rendered cross-walls act to define individual rooms and, more conventionally, as elements of fixed furniture. In combination with the shuttered-concrete soffits, as luxurious as anything at London's National Theatre, they create a house that already has a comfortable and lived-in quality.

The relationship between the front and back of the site, with views around and through the house, make this an unusually satisfying place to experience.

CLIENT PRIVATE
STRUCTURAL ENGINEER DOWNES ASSOCIATES
CONTRACTOR HILLSIDE CONTRACTS
CONTRACT VALUE £421,000
COMPLETION DATE MARCH 2003
GROSS INTERNAL AREA 280 SQUARE METRES
PHOTOGRAPHER DENNIS GILBERT – VIEW

GROUND-FLOOR PLAN

LIMERICK COUNTY HALL
.LIMERICK, IRELAND .BUCHOLZ MCEVOY

Set in the context of arterial roads, a shopping centre and a sea of suburban housing, this new civic complex is an outstanding example of how architectural skill allied to client aspiration can produce a landmark whose strength derives from a committed approach to finding a truly functional response to the brief.

A linear office building fronted by the council chamber, Limerick County Hall rises above its context, both physically and through a spirit of bravura, to impart a truly civic presence. The diagram for the building is clear and uncompromised. The internal street running behind the inclined glazed elevation of the office building has a generosity of scale and, with its open balconies to the offices above, reinforces the idea of local services that are accessible to the public.

This is a significant investment for the council, which has been mitigated by a thorough design approach to cost-in-use, particularly in relation to energy. There is virtually no air-conditioning; the environmental design has produced a dramatic use of timber louvres on the most public elevation, and a system of cross-ventilation that is straightforward and well detailed.

The temptation for architecture to translate the idea of open government too literally is avoided here. One of the main approaches to the office building runs parallel with the public viewing gallery into the council chamber. Combined with a degree of transparency, this allows the public a glimpse of the beautifully appointed chamber without turning it into a major gesture. The chamber is a model of how to combine gravitas with openness and light.

The timber louvres are a *tour de force*, giving the building a legible signature and a real presence in a sea of mediocrity. Timber is only one of many materials on show, with steel and glass, and a terracotta rainscreen on the rotunda of the chamber. But internally the building is all of a piece thanks in no small measure to the architect-designed fixtures and fittings.

CLIENT LIMERICK COUNTY COUNCIL
STRUCTURAL ENGINEER MICHAEL PUNCH & PARTNERS
SERVICES ENGINEER BURO HAPPOLD
FAÇADE ENGINEER RFR PARIS
QS BOYD CREED SWEET
CONTRACTOR JOHN SISK & CO LTD
CONTRACT VALUE £16 MILLION
COMPLETION DATE OCTOBER 2003
GROSS INTERNAL AREA 7000 SQUARE METRES
PHOTOGRAPHER MICHAEL MORAN

SHORTLISTED FOR THE RIBA SUSTAINABILITY AWARD

IJBURG BLOK
.AMSTERDAM, THE NETHERLANDS .MACCREANOR LAVINGTON

Blok 4, Maccreanor Lavington's latest building, is strategically located on the south-west corner of Amsterdam's newest island, the Ijburg. It is the first completed development of this new community of nearly 8000 homes and associated schools, shops and medical facilities. This is true urbanism in what could have been a suburban context.

The building appears as you arrive – by car, bus and eventually tram – over Grimshaw's recently completed bridge. A long, deep, four-storey block, it is generous in the volumes it offers its residents. This gives an appropriate scale to the building and allows both live and live-work units to co-exist, fulfilling both architectural and statutory requirements.

The block is constructed using the almost-ubiquitous Dutch tunnel-form construction technique. The ground floor, sitting over a basement of car parking, has, however, been adapted so that commercial uses can expand laterally in the future. The units themselves are shells, but with a clear programme identified in the architecture. On all levels you arrive in the middle of the plan. From here you can turn towards the largest volume. This opens on to large balconies, which are very generous outside rooms, and look out south over the water.

All the vertical and horizontal surfaces of the building's exterior are covered in a skilfully designed and executed system of precast, preclad, dark engineering-brick panels with movement joints concealed in the staggered joints. The result is a building that is both imposing and expressive of its materiality, a clever development in the debate on the role of structure, skin and materials.

On the day the jury visited, the large bar at the corner was established and thriving. Balconies expressed the contrasting lives of their occupants, and the building was all the better for it. Here is a building that works on an urban and an individual scale, setting an important standard for residential development in conception, detail, execution and occupation.

CLIENT WATERSTAD 1
STRUCTURAL ENGINEER VAN ECK
SERVICES ENGINEER BAM WONINGBOUW
CONTRACTOR BAM WONINGBOUW
CONTRACT VALUE £8.25 MILLION
COMPLETION DATE MAY 2003
GROSS INTERNAL AREA 9756 SQUARE METRES
PHOTOGRAPHER ANN BOUSEMA

ALSO ON STIRLING PRIZE MIDLIST

GROUND-FLOOR PLAN

181 .EUROPEAN UNION

STORTORGET
.KALMAR, SWEDEN .CARUSO ST JOHN

This project represents the lightest of touches, in terms of the visible manifestations of the designer's hand, to have presented itself as a candidate for an RIBA award, but every touch has been wonderfully judged and manages to look very simple. In fact the hard-landscape project for Kalmar's Stortorget (the main square) was made difficult and potent precisely because of what it represents for the town. It has historically been the space around which the key forces of the community gathered: religion, justice, education and administration.

Using the materials of this part of Sweden – granite setts and field stones – together with the artifice of paths made of large sections of pre-cast concrete, an abstract weave and pattern has been very subtly wrought from existing clues. Nothing is allowed to impair the purity of this vision: kerbs are maintained at a minimum, the levels for drainage and emphasis are carefully controlled and only the acoustic of the five subterranean water fountains – a highly successful collaboration with the artist Eva Löfdahl – disturbs the surface. Demarcation of the space is achieved by bollards, and another higher horizon is established with the use of slim stainless-steel shafts topped by low-level lights.

Stortorget is a magical place and the judges hoped that it will remain under civic control and free of the clutter of street furniture.

CLIENTS KALMAR KOMMUN (MATS HAGLUND)/STATENS KONSTRÅD (CATHARINA GABRIELSSON)
ARTIST EVA LÖFDAHL
CONTRACTOR KALMAR KOMMUN, GATU-OCH PARKKONTORET
CONTRACT VALUE £625,000
COMPLETION DATE APRIL 2003
GROSS AREA 14,000 SQUARE METRES
PHOTOGRAPHER HÉLÈNE BINET

PLAN

ONTARIO COLLEGE OF ART & DESIGN .TORONTO, CANADA .ALSOP ARCHITECTS WITH RYWA

Ontario College of Art & Design (OCAD) celebrated its 125th anniversary in 2003. In anticipation of this, and to accommodate the increasing contribution made to the Ontario economy by the creative industries, OCAD commissioned Alsop to expand its facilities. Once appointed, Alsop set up a series of client workshops with college staff and students, leading to the exchange not only of ideas but also of sketches. The resulting early designs were then shown to local residents and the city authorities for their input.

The resulting project is courageous, bold and just a little insane: it has been likened to a Dalmatian that has swallowed a billiard table. Predictably it evoked a strong and contradictory set of responses from the jury, but the majority commended the imaginative solution that has been developed. By elevating the new building nine storeys above the ground, land that might have been built on has been saved for shared use and turned from a car park in to an external extension of the college's activities. It also means that views from across the street to the park have been preserved, giving it a head start in the popularity stakes. The iconic nature of the design has proved to be very successful in the college's fund-raising campaign, which has exceeded its target.

The pixillated skin of the dramatic new wing is reminiscent of military camouflage schemes but in a curious inversion is designed to fragment the simple rectangular form of the building for those living and working beside and underneath it.

CLIENT ONTARIO COLLEGE OF ART & DESIGN (PETER CALDWELL)
STRUCTURAL ENGINEER CARRUTHERS & WALLACE LTD
SERVICES ENGINEER MCW CONSULTANTS
CONTRACTOR PCL CONSTRUCTORS CANADA INC
CONTRACT VALUE 42.5 CANADIAN DOLLARS
COMPLETION DATE 2004
GROSS INTERNAL AREA 7800 SQUARE METRES (ADDITION)/16,000 SQUARE METRES (RENOVATION)
PHOTOGRAPHER RICHARD JOHNSON

SECTION

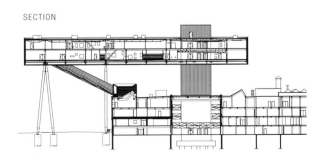

YOKOHAMA INTERNATIONAL PASSENGER TERMINAL .YOKOHAMA, JAPAN .FOREIGN OFFICE ARCHITECTS

Foreign Office Architects won the competition to design the terminal back in 1995. When the go-ahead was finally given, the architects rapidly added to the existing team what they call Japanese Sherpas (those with local knowledge) and Spanish Gurkhas (those not hidebound by local convention and capable of committing the 'worst atrocities'). The entire team then moved to Japan to carry out their mission. No building of quite this kind has been done before, so the project was grown more than designed. Teamwork and a strong culture meant that they could make do with fourteen architects instead of the thirty to forty the project managers insisted were necessary.

The brief had called not only for a passenger cruise terminal but also for a mix of facilities for local citizens, all under one roof. The architects succinctly described their proposal as a declaration to create an open public space instead of producing a monument or gate to travel. The clarity of this concept, of the roof of the building as an open plaza and extension to the nearby parks – this being the missing link in a chain of public parks along the city's waterfront – has been carried through with brave determination. It is a scheme that balances the very stringent pragmatics of a complex circulation diagram, coupled with highly technical engineering constraints, with a poetic vision that remains undiminished in execution.

Architects often use colour to differentiate spaces; here Foreign Office have limited their palette of materials and details and thrown away any distinctions between the materials used inside and out.

This is a building at the scale of civil engineering but its complexity has been mastered without the confusion that can easily overwhelm projects with such a vast array of professional requirements. The reduced material palette has led to a richness of spatial and scalar expression at each of the landscape-scaled levels. It is rare and exciting to see preachers turn to practice with such facility, and the jury was unanimous in its praise.

CLIENT CITY OF YOKOHAMA
STRUCTURAL ENGINEER STRUCTURAL DESIGN GROUP
SERVICES ENGINEER P T MORIMURA & ASSOCIATES
CONTRACTOR SHIMIZU CORPORATION (1ST DIVISION)/KAJIMA CORPORATION (2ND DIVISION)/TODA CORPORATION (3RD DIVISION)
CONTRACT VALUE £118 MILLION
COMPLETION DATE 2002
GROSS INTERNAL AREA 34,732 SQUARE METRES
PHOTOGRAPHER SATORU MISHIMA

FIRST-FLOOR PLAN

MINAMI-YAMASHIRO ELEMENTARY SCHOOL
.KYOTO, JAPAN .RICHARD ROGERS PARTNERSHIP

This low-budget scheme was designed as long ago as 1995 in response to a brief that called for a school for six- to twelve-year-olds that would also provide facilities for the community – a highly unusual combination in Japan. The building is conceived as a big house, giving the flexibility necessary for such mixed use. The detailing and implementation of the scheme were done in RRP's Tokyo office, specifying simple, durable and low-maintenance materials. The result is an elegant East-meets-West building.

The Minami-Yamashiro school impresses by the clarity and simplicity with which it converts a complex brief, not only for a school but also for a community resource, into an elegant and economic solution.

The north–south orientation was a practical response to the topography of the site, reducing the quantity of soil that had to be removed in the tight schedule permitted by the school timetable. The building is confidently disposed into two main elements, both two-storey and toplit. The simple linear composition responds to, yet strongly contrasts with, the rugged terrain.

Constructionally, the building is a clear frame-and-panel composition. The concrete frame is rigorously executed and defines the plan. In contrast, the roof panels appear to float, admitting north light into the heart of the deep-plan spaces. Walls are either glazed or strongly coloured, creating a lively counterpoint to the frame and geometry.

The relationship between teaching and circulation spaces is particularly successful, being made flexible and informal through the use of sliding screens. In addition, the project represented excellent value for money while demonstrating a meticulous attention to detail.

CLIENT YOUICHI HASHIMOTO
STRUCTURAL ENGINEER UMEZAWA STRUCTURAL ENGINEERS
SERVICES ENGINEER SETSUBI-SEKKEI 21
CONTRACTOR ASANUMA CORPORATION
LANDSCAPE ARCHITECT EQUIPE ESPACE
CONTRACT VALUE £11.8 MILLION
COMPLETION DATE 2003
TOTAL BUILDING AREA 10,235 SQUARE METRES
PHOTOGRAPHER KATSUHISA KIDA

SECOND-FLOOR PLAN

METROPOLITAN .WARSAW, POLAND .FOSTER AND PARTNERS WITH JEMS ARCHITEKCI

Foster and Partners' office building, built in collaboration with the Polish architects Jems Architekci, makes a major contribution to the re-establishment of Pilsudski Square (formerly Victory Square, an important civic space that houses the Tomb of the Unknown Soldier), as one of Warsaw's most important public spaces. The building does not try to dominate the vast square, but provides a solid anchor at one corner. Metropolitan in fact completes the square by filling in a missing side, thus defining the space within, but it does far more than this. It is a counter-balance to its historic neighbours, taking its height, materials and massing from them but without resorting to pastiche. This sensitive approach derived from a constructive dialogue with the city's historic monuments conservator.

The five-sided structure, which has a mix of shops, cafés and restaurants at ground level, unites three separate but linked office buildings into a single composition. This is organized around a central circular 50-metre-diameter courtyard that allows shortcuts across the site, making the building permeable, while also creating a clearly defined new public space complementing the square.

Façades of sheer glass maximize daylight into the offices but vertical granite fins give an apparent solidity in keeping with the building's more traditional neighbours. The fins cleverly provide a sense of solidity when viewed obliquely but transparency from head on.

Metropolitan is a building of sophisticated civility that shows how contemporary architecture can enhance the urban realm without setting out to draw attention to itself. It is a fitting contribution to Warsaw's increasingly cosmopolitan character and well befits its status as the capital of one of the most economically important members of the enlarged European Union.

(This building was ineligible for an RIBA Award as Poland was not an EU member when the 2004 Awards closed.)

CLIENT HINES POLSKA
STRUCTURAL ENGINEER WATERMAN INTERNATIONAL, AIB
SERVICES ENGINEERS ROGER PRESTON AND PARTNERS/ROGER PRESTON POLSKA
CONTRACTOR HOCHTIEF POLAND
CONTRACT VALUE CONFIDENTIAL
COMPLETION DATE 2003
GROSS INTERNAL AREA 37,080 SQUARE METRES
PHOTOGRAPHER WOJCIECH KRYNSKI

SITE PLAN

CASA FONTANA
.LUGANO, SWITZERLAND .STANTON WILLIAMS

This is a villa on a beautiful site pinned between the switchbacks of a precipitous road in the Swiss Alps. The client brief contained a number of verbal clues such as 'I work in the cool of those shading pine trees' or 'I make breakfast here looking this way'. From these word-pictures the architects built up a living diagram strung across the site, which in turn formed the basis for the final design.

The steep slope has been organized into a collection of terraces connected by a winding stepped path. Buildings are either tucked under or placed on the terraces. Secondary buildings for guests, cars and services are recessed beneath the plane of the terrace. The main house is an almost freestanding object positioned at the highest point of the site.

The principal spatial experience is the discovery of the wonderful view as you walk from the upper entrance through the main living rooms. You are drawn instinctively towards the edge, overlooking the distant peaks and valleys. The terraces act as an immediate horizon, cutting out the middle ground. The architects describe the careful framing of particular views using painstaking trial and error, but the building is really a frame for the almost infinite expanse of sky, clouds, mountains and water.

The architects' instinct is to make a quiet building that luxuriates in good materials used with tact. The strategy is one of careful placement and subtly managed circulation. The land is the primary experience, with its shady, fragrant vegetation, its geology and slowly percolating water. The shifting temperature between day and night is an agent of change that modulates the experience of the building. Everything is surrounded by great space. The house is a quiet witness to this.

CLIENT JAN ERIK LUNDBERG
STRUCTURAL ENGINEER REGOLATI E SPADEA
INTERIOR DESIGNER SHIDEH SHAYGAN
CONTRACTOR VARIOUS LOCAL CONTRACTORS
CONTRACT VALUE CONFIDENTIAL
COMPLETION DATE 2003
GROSS INTERNAL AREA 450 SQUARE METRES (HOUSE)/130 SQUARE METRES (STUDIO)
PHOTOGRAPHER PATRICK ENGQUIST

GROUND-FLOOR PLAN

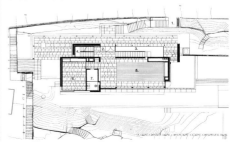

THE LOIS & RICHARD ROSENTHAL CENTER FOR CONTEMPORARY ART
.CINCINNATI, USA. ZAHA HADID ARCHITECTS

This is a contemporary art gallery built on a tight downtown corner site. It is unusually tall for a building of this kind, with public spaces on seven levels. Galleries of different sizes occupy the perimeter of the site. They are organized around an atrium that brings daylight into the back of the building and is used as a space for vertical circulation.

All the galleries are raised above ground level to allow virtually continuous direct access from the sidewalk. The fully glazed ground floor looks almost like a shopfront, but its most unusual feature is the pavement that seems to run into the building and turn up the walls, becoming a vertical backdrop to the atrium. The effect is to direct our attention to the suspended volumes of the galleries overhead.

The galleries are great solid blocks made from concrete. There are narrow gaps between each one so that it seems as though they are broken fragments of a greater whole. This contributes to the cliff-like quality that the building has by day. At night, when the building is lit internally, our perception changes. Light shines out through the fault-lines, giving them buoyancy so that, despite their apparent mass, they float free of one another. You could imagine them as a fleet of rhomboids cruising in close formation, which had simply paused for an instant on a Cincinnati street corner.

The journey up through the building exploits the drama of this interlocked matrix of mass and light. Great stepped ramps zigzag scissors-like up through the atrium space. On one side we experience the sheer concrete wall that was once the pavement. On the other, we pass up through the great tottering stack of galleries, the slots of light underlining the precarious balance. This is a visceral experience in a tough building. Here is architecture played like high drama where great mass is suspended in light.

CLIENT CONTEMPORARY ARTS CENTER
LOCAL ARCHITECT KZF DESIGN INC
SERVICES AND STRUCTURAL ENGINEER HEPY ENGINEERING
CONTRACTOR TURNER CONSTRUCTION COMPANY
CONTRACT VALUE £20.2 MILLION/£11.05 MILLION
COMPLETION DATE 2003
GROSS INTERNAL AREA 26,517 SQUARE METRES
PHOTOGRAPHERS HÉLÈNE BINE/ROLANDE HALBE (TOP RIGHT)

GROUND-FLOOR PLAN

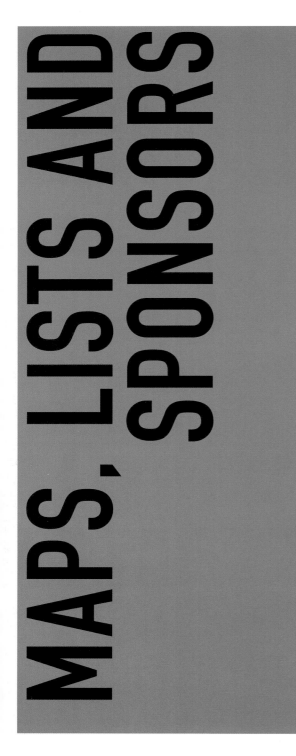

MAPS, LISTS AND SPONSORS

GREAT BRITAIN

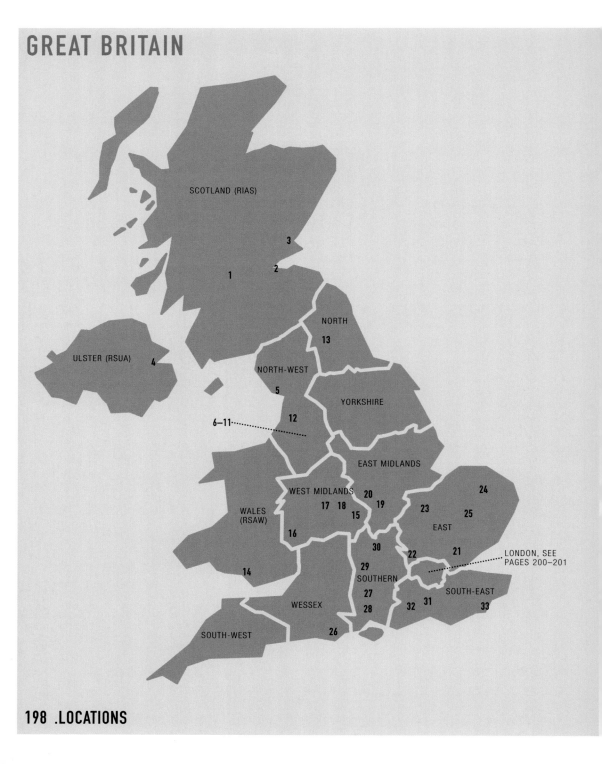

SCOTLAND (RIAS)

3

2

1

NORTH

13

ULSTER (RSUA)   4

NORTH-WEST

5

YORKSHIRE

6–11 · · · · · · · · · · · · · · · ·   12

EAST MIDLANDS

24

WEST MIDLANDS   20

17 18   19   23   25

WALES   15   EAST
(RSAW)

16   30   21

22   LONDON, SEE
14   PAGES 200–201

29   SOUTH-EAST

SOUTHERN   27   33

28   32 31

WESSEX

26

SOUTH-WEST

1   CLAVIUS BUILDING, ST ALOYSIUS COLLEGE, GLASGOW

2   DICK PLACE, EDINBURGH

3   MAGGIE'S CANCER CARING RESPITE CENTRE, NINEWELL'S HOSPITAL, DUNDEE

4   THE BATIK BUILDING, BATIK CREATIVE DESIGN STORE, THE GASWORKS, BELFAST

5   BERNERS POOL, GRANGE-OVER-SANDS

6   IMPERIAL WAR MUSEUM NORTH, MANCHESTER

7   CHINESE ARTS CENTRE, MANCHESTER

8   HOYLE EARLY YEARS CENTRE, BURY

9   THE MANCHESTER MUSEUM, THE UNIVERSITY OF MANCHESTER, MANCHESTER

10 CITY OF MANCHESTER STADIUM, MANCHESTER

11 1 PICCADILLY GARDENS, MANCHESTER

12 TFL INTERNATIONAL OFFICES, RIVERSWAY, PRESTON

13 THE MINOTAUR, KIELDER FOREST PARK VISITOR CENTRE, KIELDER

14 SKER HOUSE, BRIDGEND

15 COMPTON VERNEY MANSION, WARWICKSHIRE

16 THE MOAT, HEREFORD CATHEDRAL JUNIOR SCHOOL, HEREFORD

17 SELFRIDGES, BIRMINGHAM

18 PHOENIX INITIATIVE, COVENTRY

19 PEN GREEN CENTRE, CORBY

20 SPARKENHOE THEATRE, SPARKENHOE COMMUNITY PRIMARY SCHOOL, LEICESTER

21 ADVANCE DENTAL CLINIC, CHELMSFORD

22 BEAUFORT COURT ZERO EMISSIONS BUILDING, KINGS LANGLEY

23 THE BLACK HOUSE, PRICKWILLOW

24 THE FORUM, NORWICH

25 WAKELINS; WICKHAMBROOK

26 LIGHTHOUSE, POOLE'S CENTRE FOR THE ARTS, POOLE

27 GRANGE PARK OPERA HOUSE, NORTHINGTON

28 OSBORNE SCHOOL, WINCHESTER

29 PRIVATE ESTATE, BERKSHIRE

30 SLOANE ROBINSON BUILDING, KEBLE COLLEGE, OXFORD

31 BUTTERFLY HOUSE, DUNSFOLD

32 ROLLS-ROYCE MANUFACTURING PLANT AND HEAD OFFICE, WESTHAMPNETT

33 VISTA, DUNGENESS

LONDON

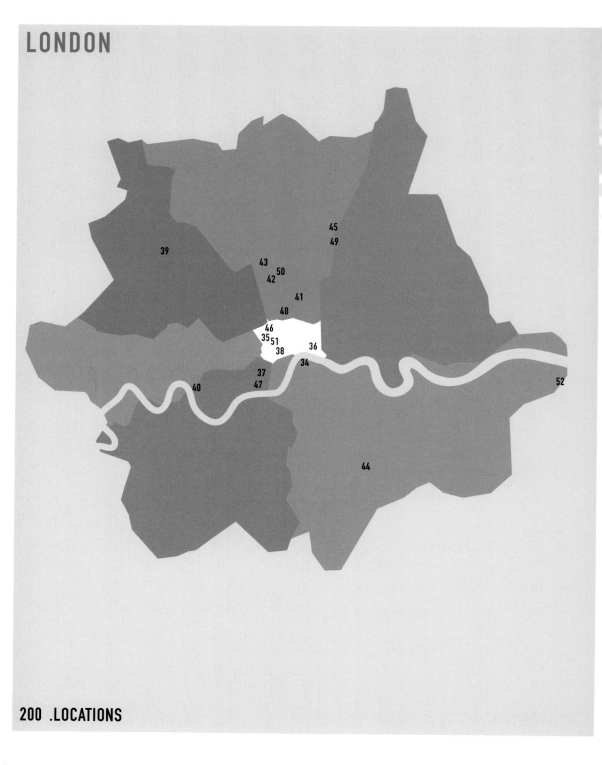

45
49

39

43
42 50

41

48

46
35 51
38   36

37   34
47

40

52

44

ASSESSORS

The RIBA is extremely grateful to the assessors, all of whom, both architects and non-architects, give their time freely and whose reports form the basis of much of the text of this book.

THE STIRLING PRIZE JURY 2004
Isabel Allen, Deborah Bull, Ted Cullinan, Antony Gormley, Francine Houben

REGIONAL ASSESSORS – RIBA AWARDS 2004
The judges are listed in the following order:
chair of jury (nationally appointed architect)/lay juror/
regional representative (architect from region)

SCOTLAND
Stephen Hodder, Laurie Taylor, James Pask

NORTHERN IRELAND
Rachel Haugh, Kenneth Powell, Clyde Markwell

NORTH-WEST
Robin Nicholson, Doreen Massey, Ian Beaumont

NORTH
Sheila O'Donnell, Jane Priestman, Guy Holmes

YORKSHIRE (no awards)
Sheila O'Donnell, Jane Priestman, Ric Blenkham

WALES
Clare Wright, Iain Tuckett, Wayne Foster

WEST MIDLANDS
Alex de Rijke, Elizabeth Minkin, Paul Lister

EAST MIDLANDS
Alex de Rijke, Elizabeth Minkin, Antony Wood

EAST
Michael Manser, Adam Sampson, Peter Goodwin

SOUTH-WEST (no awards)
Peter Jamieson, Dan Cruickshank, Bob MacDonald

WESSEX
Peter Jamieson, Dan Cruickshank, Louise Crossman

SOUTH
Gordon Benson, Anthony Bowne, David Ashe

SOUTH-EAST
Angela Brady, Caroline Cole, Bob Rathmill

LONDON SOUTH
David Morley, Simon Harris, Mary Thum

LONDON NORTH AND WEST
Ken Shuttleworth (Eric Parry), Edward Impey, Jamie Fobert

LONDON EAST
Professor Peter Cook, Peter Cook, Andrew Taylor

EUROPEAN UNION
Simon Allford, Tony Chapman, Paul Finch, Richard Griffiths,

Birkin Haward, Niall McLaughlin, Paul Monaghan, Peter Morris, Mohsen Mostafavi, David Page, Eric Parry, Jeremy Till, Joanna van Heyningen, Giles Worsley

WORLDWIDE AWARDS (NOT VISITED)
Tony Chapman, Peter Davey, Paul Finch, Glenn Howells, Niall McLaughlin, Eric Parry, Joanna van Heyningen, Giles Worsley

SPECIAL AWARDS

THE MANSER MEDAL – SPONSORED BY THE BEST OF BRITISH HOMES AND ABROCOUR
Michael Manser, George Ferguson, Jamie Fobert, Michael Hanson, David Birkbeck, Tony Chapman

THE ARCHITECTS' JOURNAL FIRST BUILDING AWARD – IN ASSOCIATION WITH ROBIN ELLIS DESIGN AND CONSTRUCTION
Robin Ellis, Barrie Evans, Alex de Rijke

THE RIBA/ARTS COUNCIL ENGLAND CLIENT OF THE YEAR
The RIBA's Award Group, chaired by Eric Parry

THE STEPHEN LAWRENCE PRIZE SPONSORED BY THE MARCO GOLDSCHMIED FOUNDATION
Marco Goldschmied, Doreen Lawrence, David Taylor

THE RIBA INCLUSIVE DESIGN AWARD – IN ASSOCIATION WITH THE CENTRE FOR ACCESSIBLE ENVIRONMENTS AND ALLGOOD
Sarah Langton-Lockton, Mike Hield, Tony Chapman

THE CROWN ESTATE CONSERVATION AWARD
Roger Bright, Richard Griffiths, David Pickles, Giles Worsley, Tony Chapman

RIBA SUSTAINABILITY AWARD – SPONSORED BY SCHÜCO
Eric Parry, Bill Dunster, Bill Gething, Tony Chapman

PREVIOUS WINNERS

STIRLING PRIZE

1996	Hodder Associates	University of Salford
1997	Michael Wilford & Partners	Music School, Stuttgart, Germany
1998	Foster and Partners	American Air Museum, Duxford
1999	Future Systems	NatWest Media Centre, Lord's, London
2000	Alsop & Störmer	Peckham Library & Media Centre, London
2001	Wilkinson Eyre Architects	Magna, Rotherham
2002	Wilkinson Eyre Architects	Millennium Bridge, Gateshead
2003	Herzog & de Meuron	Laban, Deptford, London

RIBA CLIENT OF THE YEAR

1998	Roland Paoletti
1999	The MCC
2000	The Foreign & Commonwealth Office
2001	Molendinar Park Housing Association, Glasgow
2002	Urban Splash
2003	Manchester City Council

THE STEPHEN LAWRENCE PRIZE

1998	Ian Ritchie Architects	Terrasson Cultural Greenhouse, France
1999	Munkenbeck + Marshall	Sculpture Gallery, Roche Court, Salisbury
2000	Softroom Architects	Kielder Belvedere
2001	Richard Rose-Casemore	Hatherley Studio, Winchester
2002	Cottrell + Vermeulen	Cardboard Building, Westborough School, Westcliff-on-Sea
2003	Gumuchdjian Architects	Think Tank, Skibberreen, Ireland

THE CROWN ESTATE CONSERVATION AWARD

1998	Peter Inskip & Peter Jenkins	Temple of Concord & Victory, Stowe
1999	Foster and Partners	The Reichstag, Berlin, Germany
2000	Foster and Partners	JC Decaux UK Headquarters, London
2001	Rick Mather Architects	The Dulwich Picture Gallery, London
2002	Richard Murphy Architects	Stirling Tolbooth
2003	LDN Architects	Newhailes House Conservation, Musselburgh

THE RIBA JOURNAL SUSTAINABILITY AWARD

2000	Chetwood Associates	Sainsbury's, Greenwich
2001	Michael Hopkins & Partners	Jubilee Campus, Nottingham University
2002	Cottrell + Vermeulen	Cardboard Building, Westborough School, Westcliff-on-Sea
2003	Bill Dunster Architects	BedZED, Wallington

THE ADAPT TRUST ACCESS AWARD

2001	Avery Associates Architects	Royal Academy of Dramatic Arts, London
2002	Malcolm Fraser Architects	Dance Base, Edinburgh
2003	Nicholl Russell Studios	The Space, Dundee College

THE ARCHITECTS' JOURNAL FIRST BUILDING AWARD IN ASSOCIATION WITH ROBIN ELLIS DESIGN AND CONSTRUCTION

2001	Walker Architecture	Cedar House, Logiealmond
2002	Sutherland Hussey	Barnhouse, Highgate, London
2003	De Rijke Marsh Morgan	No. 1 Centaur Street, London

THE MANSER MEDAL

2003	Jamie Fobert Architects	Anderson House, London

SPONSORS

 The RIBA is grateful to all the sponsors who make the awards possible, in particular *The Architects'
Journal*, published by Emap, the main sponsors, who provide the money for the RIBA Stirling Prize
and its judging costs. *The Architects' Journal* has been promoting good architecture since 1895. Its weekly
news coverage, comprehensive building studies, in-depth technical and practice features and incisive
commentary make it the UK's leading architectural magazine, whose authoritative voice has informed
generations of architects.

The Architects' Journal also sponsors *The Architects' Journal* First Building Award in association with Robin
Ellis Design & Construction. The prize is intended to mark the successful transition by a young practice
from interiors and small works to a complete piece of architecture.

The RIBA would also like to thank the other sponsors of the Special Awards:
The Centre for Accessible Environments, which is an information provider and a forum for collaborative
dialogue between providers and users on how the built environment can best be made or modified to
achieve inclusion by design; and Allgood, which manufactures a wide range of Disability Discrimination
Act-compliant architectural ironmongery – joint sponsors of the new RIBA Inclusive Design Award;
SCHÜCO, Europe's leading façades, curtain-walling and windows company, new sponsors of The RIBA
Sustainability Award;
Arts Council England, who have sponsored The RIBA Client of the Year from its inception in 1998. Arts
Council England is the national development agency for the arts in England, distributing public money from
Government and the National Lottery;
The Marco Goldschmied Foundation, established by RIBA past-President Marco Goldschmied, sponsors of
The Stephen Lawrence Prize, established in 1998 in memory of the murdered black teenager who aspired
to be an architect. Marco Goldschmied's foundation also supports the Stephen Lawrence Charitable Trust
and in particular its bursary programme, which helps train black architects (www.stephenlawrence.org.uk);
The Crown Estate, sponsors of The Crown Estate Conservation Award, first presented in 1998, which
manages a large and uniquely diverse portfolio of land and buildings across the UK. One of its primary
concerns is to make historic buildings suitable for today's users;
The Best of British Homes, the annual reference work of award-winning housing, showcasing exemplars of
best design practice, published by Emap; and Abrocour, which provides the wireless IT fixtures and fittings
to new homes, joint sponsors of The Manser Medal.

All RIBA Award winners receive a lead plaque produced and donated by the Lead Sheet Association, to be placed on the building. The LSA is the primary independent body involved in the promotion and development of the use of rolled-lead sheet. The LSA offers authoritative technical advice and comprehensive training services to ensure that rolled-lead sheet maintains its matchless reputation as one of the most-established long-lasting and environmentally friendly construction materials. The LSA is proud to have been associated with the RIBA Awards since 1989.

The RIBA would also like to thank the sponsors of the RIBA Stirling Prize Presentation Dinner:
DP9, London's leading town-planning consultants;
Formica, the UK market leader in high-pressure laminate. Formica is the 'original' and continues to lead the field in terms of innovation and design;
Pendock – suppliers of decorative architectural casings solutions for structural columns and interior M&E services;
SCHÜCO, Europe's leading façades, curtain-walling and windows company. It prides itself on its innovative 'total solutions' approach for large or small projects, which includes renewable-energy systems;
SIV Executive, the industry's pre-eminent recruitment service and creative business team, who co-ordinate exclusive assignments and introductions for senior-level architectural individuals and clients.
Thanks also to Fusion Glass Designs, suppliers of structural, architectural and decorative glass, who designed, produced and donated the glass panels for the Stirling presentation set.

The RIBA would also like to thank Channel 4 for their continuing coverage of The RIBA Stirling Prize in association with *The Architects' Journal*.

PHOTOGRAPHS The RIBA would also like to thank all the photographers whose work is published in this book and who are credited in the main text for agreeing to waive copyright fees for reproduction by the RIBA of their work in connection with the promotion of the RIBA Awards.

INDEX